'Alphabet Se

'Alphabet': The Almigh

Phoenician Guide to the Process of Self- Creation

'Alphabet': Twenty-Two Steps to Enlightenment

Inner Journey through the Sacred Phoenician Alphabet
revealing the 'Story of Creation', 'Kabbalah', 'Astrology', and 'Tarot'

Cover designed by Christine Brydon and Edward Adamthwaite:

Whatsme: Designs & Collections | Zazzle.co.uk

ISBN   978-3-7497-4195-3 (Paperback)
ISBN   978-3-7497-4196-0 (eBook)

'ALPHABET'

The Twenty-Two Steps to Enlightenment

'Inner Journey through the Sacred Phoenician Alphabet revealing the 'Story of Creation', Kabbalah, Astrology, and Tarot'

by Christine Brydon M.A.

Published by 'tredition'
GmbH, Hamburg, Germany

This manual is a companion volume to 'Alphabet':
The Almighty Word Within:
(Phoenician Guide to the Process of Self-Creation)
(Christine Brydon: 2018).

Table of Contents

3

In his search for truth Marcel Proust discovered:

"A pair of wings, a different mode of breathing, which would enable us to traverse infinite space, would in no way help us, for, if we visited Mars or Venus keeping the same senses, they would clothe in the same aspect as the things of the earth everything that we should be capable of seeing".

The only true voyage of discovery, the only fountain of Eternal Youth, would be not to visit strange lands but to possess other eyes, to behold the universe through the eyes of another, of a hundred others, to behold the hundred universes that each of them beholds, each of them is."

Marcel Proust: 'In Search of Lost Time', Vol 5: *The Prisoner:* originally published in French. *1923*

4

Preface

The first Manual in the Alphabet series, 'Alphabet: The Almighty Word Within' (*Brydon 2018*), is an introduction to the origin, function, and purpose of the Mysterious Symbols and Letters of the Sacred Phoenician Alphabet. While this second Manual describes in more detail how we might use the Sacred Letters to elevate our conscious awareness by looking at various traditions and stories, which are alleged to have been inspired by the original Sacred Alphabet. These include the 'Story of Creation' according to the Book of Genesis in the Bible, 'The Mystical Kabbalah', the 'Art of Astrology', Tarot, and their association with Colour. For although these subjects may appear to be divergent, they are all based on, or reveal the 'Process of Self-Creation' which transpires within us while on our Journey to our Divine Destination. However, the true nature of the original intention of these stories and legends has been greatly modified by subsequent generations to reflect the cultural practices and perceptions which were prevalent in the lives of the people at the time that the original stories were being re-told.

The Sacred Phoenician Alphabet is the first phonetic alphabet in the western world which associates symbols, or pictographs with sound, thought to have been devised over 4000 years ago by ancient Canaanites who eventually became known as the Inimitable Phoenicians. Nevertheless, no one really knows where the

6

Mysterious Symbols and Letters of the Sacred Alphabet actually originated, but the ancient Canaanites maintained that the Sacred Alphabet was 'Conceived' by the Self-Reproducing God-dess of Pure Light, who had descended to Earth from the Stars. Hence, the Canaanites regarded the Sacred Alphabet as a Magical System to guide Seekers through the 'Process of Self-Creation' in Twenty-Two Steps, to a State of Enlightenment, by forming words with the resonant sounds of the Sacred Letters. And the Canaanites narrated the Miraculous Stories concerning the Celestial Origins of the Magical Universe, revealed to them by the Inner Star Seed of Light.

Hence, since the letters of our modern alphabet, which has its roots in the Phoenician Sacred Alphabet, are used to form words to tell, and re-tell our own personal stories and dramas, these Mysterious Symbols, which are alleged to have been devised by the Celestial Ancestors of the ancient Canaanites, continue to 'conjure up' the appearance of Miracles in the world in which we live today, if we have eyes to see. For the sensational feelings induced within us when the Sacred Letters are Spoken with Resonance and Intention, are impressed as patterns of on the DNA in our body, and influence how we perceive the world around us. Since everything that we see before us is only a reflection of the vibrations stored as memories within us that forms our 'Identity', and with which we habitually relate to as being our 'reality' in the physical world of shadows.

7

We begin our Epic Journey of Self-Discovery by reviewing the function and purpose of the Twenty-Two Symbols of the Sacred Phoenician Alphabet, and our often-confused understanding of the meaning of 'Enlightened Consciousness'. We then examine the connection between 'Consciousness', the 'Sacred Alphabet', and the 'Seven Days of Creation', as described in Genesis in the Bible, according to the Mechanical Translation of Genesis (*Benner 2007*). The Mechanical Translation of Genesis differs from the King James Version (*KJV*), or other versions of the Bible, in that it gives the original root meaning of each word, and not the personal interpretation of a word, according to the translator.

In the Mechanical Translation of Genesis, we discover that the original Hebrew transcript of the Bible has different meanings and connotations than what we had previously believed. For instance, instead of "God Said Let There Be Light", as it does in the KJV, these same words are mechanically translated as "The Power/s (*Elohiym*) Said "Light Exits", that changes a 'Command' into a 'Declaration'. For each 'Day of Creation' revealed in Genesis represents a Stage in the 'Process of our Self-Creation' through our own 'Declaration', as we consciously grow in 'Self-Knowledge'. And once we learn that 'Consciousness' means 'Self-Knowledge', we realise that what we are striving for is to return to the State of Pure Light, as it is 'Within the Beginning', which is not a 'Time' but the 'Place of Creation'.

Nevertheless, although only Pure Light is 'conceived to exist' Within the Beginning, Genesis in the Bible then tells the story of Adam and Eve and their removal from the Garden of Eden after committing the 'Original Sin' of eating the forbidden fruit from the 'Tree of Discernment', which is alleged to have caused the 'Fall of Humanity' from Heaven to Earth. Thus, each successive generation would suffer, and work hard to make a living. But to counteract this prediction, the Hebrews later devised the stories of Kabbalah and Astrology to show Humanity the 'Way' back to our Immortal State of Grace in the Pure Radiant Light of Paradise.

The 'Mystical Kabbalah' is an ancient Jewish Teaching known as the 'Way of Wisdom' through Receiving Knowledge from the Spirit within our own Heart. And contrary to popular belief, Kabbalah is not a religion, but a philosophy, based on the 'Tree of Life' that we must ascend to cause the Celestial Light which is conceived 'Within the Beginning', to descend from Heaven to Earth. However, Kabbalah conceals many hidden meanings that many 'would be' translators have tried to explain, and have in the process greatly confused its original simple conception, which was attributed to the Patriarch Abraham around 1800BC in the 'Sefer Yetzriah', (Book of Creation). Hence, the story of the 'Mystical Kabbalah' has now become too complex to be fully understood without much dedicated research and inner guidance. But the Kabbalah was originally meant to be a simple set of instructions to teach us how we can reclaim our Ancestral Birth Right as the Ruler of our own Kingdom, and to Inherit the 'Divine Wisdom' and 'Knowledge' of the Magical Light, which is already inherent within us at birth.

Similarly, the story of Astrology was adapted to tell the legend of the 'Sun', who is the 'Son' of a Divine Being on his Journey through the Zodiac to take up his rightful place as a Divine Ruler, since the Sun (Son) is considered to be Heir to the Kingdom of Heaven; hence the reason why Humanity has always told stories of the miraculous attributes of the Stars and Planets. Therefore, Astrology not only reveals the 'Way of Wisdom' to our Paradise on Earth, but also how to evaluate the Perfect Virtues and Pure Consciousness of a future King; since a King was thought to be descended from Star People of Pure Light who possessed Incredible Magical Knowledge, which a future King was assumed to have inherited at birth. Thus, our present understanding of Astrology as a fortune telling devise, in no way resembles the original story, which was devised by ancient people to guide 'Humanity' through the 'Process of Self- Creation'. For the Pure Consciousness of the Planets and Perfect Virtues of the Zodiac are impressed on the DNA of all Humanity at birth, and will lead us to our Divine Destination, once we are aware of our own Celestial Birth Right, which is the Magical Power of continuous Self-Reproduction.

The study of Astrology was initially reserved for the eyes and ears of a Priest, or someone with knowledge of the portents of the Stars. Hence, it was assumed that if a King had Inherited the 'Knowledge of Magic' at birth, then his legacy would be reflected throughout the whole Kingdom; for according to ancient Wisdom, that which is born at a specific moment shares the same quality of vibration that is evident in the Universe at that moment, which will continue to influence the world of that person. More recently the study of Astrology has become available to everyone, and our Astrological birth chart can help us understand our own personal Virtues which are impressed as a pattern on our DNA at the moment of our birth, and form the sensations we now feel in our body that influence our Self-Identity through our emotions and thoughts, which continue colour our world. For all colours are frequencies of vibration that are induced within us by the resonant Sounds of the Sacred Letters, through the Signs of the Zodiac, and Planets, which can be changed when we 'Speak the Word' to alter the sensations we are now feeling, and will transform our present perception of 'reality'.

Similar to Kabbalah and Astrology, the story of 'Tarot', describes our Inner Journey from 'Ignorance' to our Divine Destination, which is a State of Enlightenment or Self-Realisation. But it is alleged that 'Tarot' was first devised in Egypt, and has only recently become associated with the Twenty-Two Letters of the Sacred

11

Phoenician Alphabet. Of course, no one knows where the 'Tarot' actually has its roots, but it is included in this Manual because of its association with our Divine Journey, even though the order in which the Twenty-Two Cards of the Major Arcane of the Tarot are now presented follow a different sequence than the Letters of the Sacred Phoenician Alphabet. However, the Tarot reveals that our own personal Life Story is reversible, and that the route of our own Divine Journey is not decided until we ourselves perceive it is so.

Although the modest amount of information given in this Manual, concerning the modern concepts of the 'Mystical Kabbalah', 'Astrology', and 'Tarot', is not extensive, it is sufficient to help us appreciate the association between the Twenty-Two Letters of the Sacred Alphabet and the 'Elevation of Consciousness', through our knowledge of the original intention of the aforementioned subjects. For as with any 'Search for Truth', if our basic understanding of a subject is flawed, then it will not be easy to obtain meaningful answers to our most heartfelt questions. And if our understanding of Ancient Wisdom is only founded on the information acquired from modern literature, or the Internet, it will possibly cause more confusion than clarity; for in much of the modern literature today the original story has been altered many times since its conception, but nevertheless is now accepted as being 'true' by most people. Thus, this is the situation when studying the Letters of the Sacred

12

Alphabet, Consciousness, the Seven Days of Creation, Kabbalah, Astrology, and Tarot, because we have no reliable source of information on which to build our knowledge and understanding upon, and therefore must turn within to access the Wisdom of our Soul Mate which dwells within our Heart. And once we are in possession of the 'Knowledge' which will guide us to our Divine Destination, we will begin to perceive 'Reality', through new eyes.

The Magical Universe is 'Pure Vibrant Energy', which only appears to be solid to our present state of consciousness, hence, we can change our 'reality' by pronouncing the sounds of each Letter of the Sacred Alphabet to induce different vibrations in our body. For everything in existence is constantly moving at various velocities, which appears as material objects when vibrating at a slower rate of frequency, and as Pure Light when moving at a higher velocity. The frequency of our own personal vibration is controlled by the sensations that we now feel within us, produced by the sound of the words which we speak and hear; hence, we are all story tellers, creating our 'reality' through our own Declarations. But while conscious of living in a physical body, we tend to vibrate at a slower frequency until we realise that the original stories of 'Kabbalah', 'Astrology', and 'Tarot' can help us to change our rate of vibration. Since they all teach us that we must devise our own Life Story, by shifting our attention from our present world, and to focus on the

Treasures which are already stored in our Heaven. For although our Divine Destination is already assured, it depends on the stories we tell, and believe are 'true', while on our Journey of Self-Discovery, which will enhance, or impede our progress.

Thus, by repeating the sound of words with resonance we impress new vibrations on the DNA in our body which will change our Identity at a cellular level. And according to Ancient Wisdom, it is our own Self-Identity that is the most important factor when working with the Divine Magical Energy of the Cosmos. In recent years the theory of a 'Quantum Reality' supports the teachings of Ancient Wisdom, which suggest that what we perceive to be our 'reality', manifests as an apparent physical materialisation in our world. Therefore, as we alter our present vibration we grow in consciousness, which will change the reflection of what we now see and experience in the world around us; since our world is only a mirror image, or the shadow of our own self-conceptions.

Finally a précis of the Twenty-Two Symbols and Letters of the Sacred Phoenician Alphabet, the 'Seven Days of Creation', the 'Mystical Kabbalah', 'Art of Astrology', 'Tarot' and the vibration of Colour, are brought together toward the end of the Manual, under the heading 'The Twenty-Two Steps of the Process of Self-Creation', which gives a step by step account of our Inner Journey from 'Embryo to Enlightenment'. Therefore, by inducing physical sensations in our body, which are produced by the sounds of the Spoken Letters of the Sacred Alphabet, we will experience the Pure Conscious State of existing, while not existing in any particular physical form, as a 'Perfect Being of Pure Magical Light'.

For while in this Enlightened State of Pure Consciousness, which is synonymous with the Phoenician Symbol of **SIMS** that is never spoken, and therefore is not mentioned in the 'Process of Self-Creation', we understand the true meaning of the 'Silence' within our own Heart. And now fully aware of what it means to be in a 'State of Grace', we realise that all which really 'exits' 'is the 'Pure Radiant Light of Possibility'. Thus, as we 'let go' of our present misconceptions, our perception of 'reality' changes as our connection with the Pure Magical Light within us grows stronger.

Throughout the text the Bible is referred to often, which is not to promote any particular religious persuasion, but to compare the significance of the 'Story of Creation' in the Bible with the original Intention of the Symbols of the Sacred Phoenician Alphabet, that incidentally were devised long before the 'Story of Creation' in Genesis was written. For the Sacred Alphabet was 'created' by an ingenious people who in the Bronze Age worshiped the Eternal Presence of the God-dess of Pure Light and True Magic, that is both

Mother and Father of All Creation. Hence, the word 'God-dess' is hyphenated throughout the text as a reminder of the androgynous nature of the Self-Reproducing Power of Light which is forever within us wherever we are in our Magical Universe. Also, many words are capitalised to show their importance when studying the Magical Arts. For it is not the academic connotation, or grammatical precision of a Word that is being considered in this work, but the Magical Sensation that is induced within our Heart and Body when a Word is Heard, or is Spoken with Resonance and Intention.

The Sacred Phoenician Alphabet Symbols and Letters

1.		AL	12.		LAM
2.		BET	13.		MAH
3.		GAM	14.		NUN
4.		DAL	15.		SIN
5.		HEY	16.		AYIN
6.		VAV	17.		PEY
7.		ZAN	18.		TSAD
8.		HHETS	19.		QUPH
9.		THET	20.		RESH
10.		YAD	21.		SHIN
11.		KAPH	22.		TAV

The Spoken Word

The telling of stories and legends through the spoken word to describe the 'Mysteries of Life' has been practiced by all cultures since the appearance of Humanity on earth. And the 'Story of Creation', the Mystical Kabbalah, and Astrology, are just three examples of these arcane narrations which were only relatively recently recorded in writing; since before 2000BC only cuneiform script was used in Mesopotamia to tell the colourful stories of the people. One of the oldest legends is the 'Epic of Gilgamesh', King of Uruk who possessed superhuman strength, being two-thirds God inherited from his mother, and one-third human from his father. And after many heroic battles in the world, Gilgamesh finally goes in search of immortality, which is the story that most other Mesopotamian legends are founded upon.

One such legend is that of the God-dess *Namma*, which means 'Cosmic Subterranean Waters', or 'Cosmic Ocean', who was known throughout Mesopotamia for her Magical skills. For *Namma* is the androgynous, Virginal Mother Goddess who had no need of a male in order to conceive offspring, since the Magical Power of Self-Reproduction dwelled within *Namma*; thus, perhaps leading to the assumption that the 'Cosmic Creator' is asexual or androgynous in nature. The Legend of *Namma* goes on to describe the story of the God-dess giving birth to *Anki*, and his sister *Ninmah*, who are made

17

in the androgynous Image of *Namma,* and are delegated the task of creating Humanity. But after falling from grace, every human born to *Ninmah* was considered as 'weak', 'feeble', and 'malfunctioning', until *Anki,* gave them 'Bread', which is the 'Magical Essence of Life' inherited by *Anki* from his Mother, that would miraculously sustain all ailing humans while on the journey through the physical world.

However, according to the Creation Story devised by the ancient Canaanites who had lived along the coast of Phoenicia since before 7000B.C, now modern day Lebanon, the Virginal God-dess of Pure Light was known as *Ba'alat Gebal or Gebel,* who is Queen of the Border of all which appears to be manifest on Earth. And *Ba'alat Gebal* is the 'Magical Process of Self-Creation' which Immaculately Conceived, and gave birth to the Perfect Son, *Ba'al,* which means *'Lord'*, and translates as *'Staff of the Pure Light of EL Within'*, who is 'the Sustainer of Life', and the equivalent of *Anki,* who was still worshipped as the God of Nature and Thunder throughout much of Mesopotamia. Thus, *Anki* and *Ba'al,* are synonymous figures, made in the Image of the Self-Reproducing, Mother God-dess who is both male and female united as one. Hence, it is *Ba'al,* the Perfect Son of the androgynous *Ba'alat Gebal,* who the Phoenicians knew as the Pure Spirit which dwells within each human, and through *Ba'al* the Phoenicians were in constant communion with the Mother God-dess of Pure Light, in order to receive the 'Bread of Heaven'.

18

The Phoenician legend tells the story from 'Within the Beginning', which is not a moment in time, but the Silent Sanctuary within the womb of the Celestial God-dess, *Ba'alat Gebal*, where the 'Light of Pure Consciousness' is 'Immaculately Conceived' through the Mystical Union of 'Sensation' and the 'Self-Knowing Word of Perfection'. Thus, from this union an 'Immortal Child' is Immaculately Conceived, which is *Ba'al* who forever remains One with the Self-Reproducing Mother in Heaven. And Humanity is the Immortal Child which is Immaculately Conceived Within the Beginning, to bear witness to the Glory of the Celestial God-dess. But we are no longer aware of our Magical Heritage which is bequeathed to us through our Celestial Mother; for we perceive Heaven and Earth as being divided, and have forgotten that we are already living in Paradise. Hence, now feeling the sensation of being confined in a physical body we are only conscious of separation and death; deceived by our own self-reflection which appears to be our only 'reality' in the physical world of shadows.

According to the Phoenicians it was the God-dess, *Ba'alat Gebal*, who conceived the Sacred Alphabet before 'Time' began, and formed the Magical Universe by combining the Sacred Symbols and Letters to 'Spell the Word' which Declared that 'Pure Light Exists in the Perfect Image of Humanity'. And this is the origin of the term 'Magical Spells', which is the spelling of words to cause

Magical effects to appear in the world. For each Sacred Symbol represents the sound of a Letter, which when heard or spoken with resonance will induce vibrations within us that are mysteriously reflected in our world. However, the Sacred Symbols which were originally devised to produce only benign effects in our world, were eventually adapted by other cultures to tell their own stories; often of darkness, desolation, and destruction.

Henceforth, the beneficent *Anki* and *Ba'al*, who gave 'Bread' to humans to heal and sustain them, was accused by the Israelites of inciting the people to commit atrocities against the Almighty God *EL*. And the name of *Anki* and *Ba'al* was changed to *Yahweh* in the Hebrew Story of Creation, which means *I Am, or To Be*. And *Yahweh*, who is the androgynous Son, made in the Perfect Image of the Celestial God *EL*, was instructed to populate the Earth. Thus, *Yahweh* is said to have formed the man *Adam*, meaning *'Red Earth or Moving Blood'*, from the dust of the ground before breathing the 'Breath of Life' into his body. But *Adam*, who was meant to tend the Garden of Eden, fell asleep and dreamed that *Yahweh* had taken a rib from his body to form *Eve*, which means *Living*. Hence, *Adam* and *Eve* are not two separate entities, but one androgynous being; since Eve had been created from the DNA of *Adam*. However, after eating the forbidden fruit, and blaming his ill-considered actions on *Eve*, *Adam*, knowing he had disobeyed *Yahweh*, felt 'shame' and

20

'guilt' for being naked. Thus, from that moment all humans are said to be 'born in sin'; since they deny their Celestial Heritage and are deceived into believing they are confined in a material world where they will suffer pain and sorrow until death overcomes them. At which point they will return to the dust from whence they came.

That is until, so the story goes, *Moses* heard the voice of *Yahweh* who spoke of the 'Promised Land of Milk and Honey' in which the Israelites would dwell in peace and prosperity if they kept the Commandments of *Yahweh*. And *Yahweh* gave 'Manna' (*Bread of Life*) to the Israelites to heal and sustain them while wandering in the desert. And interestingly the words '*Manna*' and '*Namma*', who is the original Magical Mother Goddess of the Cosmic Ocean according to the original Mesopotamian Story of Creation, are 'spelled' with the same Letters, and therefore '*Manna*' must have similar magical qualities to *Namma*, the Mother of all Creation. And some Jewish traditions still teach that a Kosher Jew must be born of a Jewish mother in order to be considered Jewish; for the Magical quality inherent in each individual is only inherited through the mitochondrial DNA of the maternal blood line.

But in order to turn the people away from the old religion, the Israelites devised several scandalous stories to discredit the name of the Phoenicians, along with the androgynous God-dess and her

21

perfect son *Ba'al*. Thus, the God-dess *Ba'alat Gebal* was replaced by a 'God of Judgement', and Heaven was now a far-off place which could only be aspired to in the Afterlife. However, according to some authorities, the only atrocity committed by the Phoenicians, who were then living life in peace and prosperity while navigating the world in their magnificent vessels, is that they did not embrace the same religious doctrines as the Hebrews. However, the ancient Phoenicians did recognize **EL**, *the Almighty Powers of Elohiym*, as being the source of all True Magical Power, since the name of their Goddess is *Ba'(AL)at Geb(AL)*, and **AL** is the first Letter of the Sacred Phoenician Alphabet, which can also be pronounced as *EL*. And *EL* or *AL* is a shortened version of '*Elohiym*', which is plural in form but with a singular connotation.

Similarly, the teachings of early Christianity suggest that *Jesus Christ* is also synonymous with *Anki*, *Ba'al*, and *Yahweh*, and is androgynous in nature. Thus, Jesus the man became '*Christ the Redeemer*' when united with the Celestial Spirit within him. And *Christ*, like *Alki*, *Ba'al*, and *Yahweh*, is called '*Lord*', who gives the 'Bread of Life' to all weak and feeble humans, and they were all Immaculately Conceived by a Virgin Mother who was self-impregnated by the Invisible Holy Spirit. Therefore, the *Virgin Mary* is synonymous with *Namma* and *Ba'alat Gebal* of ancient legend. But Christianity is founded on the 'Holy Trinity', which is

22

'One Divine Being', comprising of the *Father*, who is *Yahweh* (*Jehovah*), the Son who is *Christ*, and the *Holy Ghost*, that is the Magical Essence of the Invisible God-dess, or the Almighty *Elohiym* (*EL*) which Declared that only 'Light Existed' Within the Beginning. And '*Christ*', who miraculously heals all humans who are suffering pain in the world, is the Ascended body of Jesus, who is now One with the Word of His *Father Jehovah/Yahweh*, and the *Holy Ghost* of His *Mother*, thus reflecting only the Pure Light in Heaven on Earth, *Christ* Rules the World by the Magical Power of His Spoken Word.

And when Christians ingest the 'Bread of Life' and 'Wine from the Vine, (*the blood line*) of Jesus, which is Mystically Transformed by the Magical Spoken Word, they partake of the Perfect Blood and Body of *Christ the Risen One*, and are 'Re-Born' to a Miraculous Life in Paradise; free from the delusions of 'shame' and 'guilt'. Thus, Jesus fulfilled the prophesy in Isaiah 7:14-16, that a Son would be born of a Virgin, and his name would be '*Immanuel*', meaning 'God is With Us', and he will refuse 'evil' and choose 'good'. But the natural response of Jesus, being One with *Christ* within him, was not to see darkness, only a Perfect Humanity. Thus, Jesus taught his disciples to eat only the nourishing fruit from the 'Tree of Life', so that Humanity might regain the 'Consciousness of Pure Light', and return to the Garden of Eden in Paradise. And in this Elevated State of Consciousness, True Christians never perceive the limitations of this world, but see and speak only of the Treasures in Heaven. Incidentally, some theologians believe that 'Jesus' was never born as a physical man, but is a representation of the 'Word' which declared "Light Exists" Within the Beginning, as is suggested in chapter 1: 1-4 of the Gospel according to the Apostle St John:

1."In the Beginning was the Word, and the Word was God. 2. The same was in the Beginning with God. 3. All things were made by him; and without him was not anything made that was made. In him was life; and the life was the Light of men." 14. "And the Word was made flesh, and dwelt among us".

Nevertheless, if Jesus was a man, he may not have been of Jewish descent, but of Phoenician lineage, since Jesus was known as 'The Nazarene', which is a word of Canaano-Phoenician origin *(Nazir);* meaning 'Keep the Word'. Added to this, Jesus himself always denied he was a Jew, and the Jews denounced Jesus for not being Jewish. But having spent most of his life in or around Jerusalem, which was originally a settlement called Ben Salem, founded by ancient Canaanites around 1900B.C., and was re-named Jerusalem by the Israelites much later, Jesus would be well versed in both Canaanite and Jewish Law. Thus, before the name 'Christianity' was devised, the people who Spoke the 'Word of Immanuel' were known as the 'Sect of Nazarenes' who adhered to the Phoenician

24

Principles of 'True Love' and 'Forgiveness'. Hence, the name 'Christian' may originally have been a derogatory term used by the Romans for the Nazarenes; since 'Christ' means 'Messiah' or 'Anointed One', and the Romans may have thought it an afront to the 'gods' that Jesus, son of a carpenter, was regarded as a Messiah. Nevertheless, the Romans went from persecuting Christians, to persecuting people for not being Christian, once Christianity had been adapted, and became the official religion of Rome in 313 A.D.

Eventually, the ideologies of the Nazarenes, who were by now becoming a threat to law and order in the Roman Empire, were amalgamated with several other popular religious beliefs of that era to form one religion, which would ensure the Romans re-gained control of the people. But the teachings of 'Jesus the Nazarene' were far more in keeping with those of the ancient Phoenicians, who taught the Principles of Peace, True Love, Forgiveness, Miraculous Healings, and the 'Oneness of Humanity, living in the Pure Magical Light in the womb of the androgynous Mother God-dess, than they were with Hebrew Ideology and Dogma of duality and darkness.

However, regardless of if the Son of the Virgin Mother is known as *Anki, Ba'al, Yahweh, Jesus Christ, Pure Consciousness, or the Word,* they all refer to the Celestial Spirit of our Soul Mate which dwells within us, which cannot be found anywhere in the outer world. And the

25

only desire of our Soul Mate is that we should experience the Divine Sensation, and Pure Consciousness of our Perfect and Immortal Self, and to reveal our own Paradise on Earth. Therefore, the Story of Christianity appears to be the re-telling of an ancient Mesopotamian legend which tells the story of our Magical Celestial origins, and the Virgin Mother God-dess of Pure Light who Immaculately Conceived the Perfect Son, in the form of Humanity, with some Roman and Hebrew stories added for good measure.

There are many such Legends which tell similar stories of our Celestial Birth Right and subsequent earthly demise, until we choose to partake of the 'Magical Bread of Life', given freely by our Divine Spirit within, which heals and sustains us. And these stories that were originally passed from mouth to ear by the Spoken Word, pre-date the written Hebrew Bible by several hundred centuries. Yet although the characters in each story have different names, they continue to play their part to reveal our own version of the Never-Ending Story, or Cosmic Drama that we call 'Life'. Thus, equating the Stories of Creation to ourselves we find that our ability to continually re-new and reproduce our 'self' comes from the Almighty Power of the Spirit which dwells within us. Since it is through this Inner Light that we can replicate our self in the Image of any form we choose, when we feel the sensation in the cells of our body, and are conscious of existing in this state in the world.

This Miraculous ability is said to be the result of the intervention of a Celestial Magical Being of Extra-Terrestrial origin, who allegedly passed on a 'Cosmic Gene' to Humanity. And this is the reason for mankind's sudden leap in evolution in comparison with other animals; which is the story told by countless ancient civilizations through the world. Amazingly, there may be some evidence to support these ancient legends, since geneticists have discovered that our DNA contains several genes of unknown origin, known as 'Ghost' DNA. And since they don't know where these genes originate, they could hold the key to solving the mystery of the origins of Humanity; for many parts of our DNA lie dormant, and ironically, they will not be activated until we become conscious of these 'Otherworldly' sensations in the ells of our body, through the Magical Power of our own Spoken Word.

Normal Human Nuclear DNA contains the information stored in twenty-three pairs of chromosomes which are inherited from both parents at our conception. And twenty-two pairs of chromosomes regulate the functioning of our organs, while chromosomes 23 determine our sex or gender. And while a female only has XX chromosomes, a male has X and Y; thus, depending on whether the X or Y chromosome is passed from the male during conception, will determine the gender, or sexual characteristics of the child. Hence, the presence of XX or XY chromosomes in our body determines if

27

we appear female on the outside and male on the inner, or visa versa; since we are 'Whole' androgynous beings who only outwardly appear to be either male or female.

Although only one X chromosome is functioning in a female, while the other X chromosome lies dormant, known as X-inactivation, the X chromosome which is functional carries most of the genetic information to keep our body functioning properly. However, it is the Mitochondrial DNA, which is only passed to embryos of both sexes through the mother, which regulates our metabolism. Thus, it is the mtDNA which bestows upon Humanity the miraculous ability to change the Light in the air we breathe, and food we eat, into a usable form of vital energy to reproduce the cells in our body. And even though males carry the X chromosomes, the male has inherited this X chromosome from his mother. This process is known as the 'Genesis of Eve'; since every human inherits the miraculous ability to change 'Ethereal Light' into physical form, inherited from the X chromosome of Eve, but only females can give birth to another human being in the world.

Even so, as a man become more 'Enlightened', because of his personal experiences in the world, he gradually becomes aligned with the Female aspect of his Inner Spirit until eventually they become One, which is a 'Marriage Made in Heaven'. And when a man continues to be nourished by the Pure Feminine energy within him, he will become the Emperor of his own world, naming all things which he desires to become manifest. Thus, when a man takes a wife, she is the reflection of his relationship with his Inner Feminine Spirit, with whom he has taken a Vow to remain constantly united. And if the man has a loving relationship with his Divine Inner Counterpart, he will experience the same affectionate partnership with his earthly wife. But if a man has not yet formed a connection with his Inner Divinity, then he will not find the reflection of his own 'True Love' in the world. For our partner only reflects, or mirrors the relationship that we have with our Inner Self.

This is also true of women, who often have no conception of the Power of their Masculine Inner Spirit. But as a female goes through the three stages of 'Womanhood'; from 'Maiden', to 'Mother', then to 'Crone' after the menopause, her relationship with her Inner Masculine Spirit is strengthened. For during the menopause, which is known as 'The Change of Life', women physically go through a metamorphosis, and the 'hot flushes' are a catalyst which transform the functioning of the cells in her body. Thus, in keeping with the androgynous, Self-Reproducing, God-dess of Pure Light, a 'Crone' is Self-Impregnated by the 'Power of the Word' of the Divine Spirit, and she gives birth to her own Inner Light in the world.

Nevertheless, women today are often so engrossed by the terrible stories they hear about the menopause that they sadly miss the opportunities that this 'time of life' gives us. But as Humanity wakes up, we will re-gain the 'Wisdom' of the 'Old Ways', and women will re-claim their own Divine Heritage; not by fighting for equality with men, but by acknowledging their own Unique Inner Power, which comes from the 'Magical Star Seed of Self-Reproduction' already inherent within her at the moment of birth; which is activated through the sensations induced in the body by the resonant sound of her own Spoken Word. Thus, the 'Wisdom' concerning the roles of males and females, has been passed on through the Stories told by the Phoenicians, and other Ancient People who lived in egalitarian societies, where the 'Wisdom of Women' was acknowledged, and highly regarded.

For it is by telling and listening to stories that we become 'Enlightened', which means to be more informed, aware, and have greater knowledge and understanding of our self and the world in which we now live. But ironically, we are only ever 'Conscious' of our own self-image in the outer world, which is our 'Magical Mirror' that only reflects the true image of our own inner nature. For the sensations we feel which are produced by the sounds of the words that we Speak and Hear are mysteriously revealed in our world as manifestations, according to our state of consciousness.

The Written Word

The first book thought to have been recorded in phonetic script, which associates sound with written letters, is the *'Sefer Yetzirah'*, or 'Book of Creation' that was attributed to the Patriarch Abraham around 1800BC. However, given the tradition in the Bronze Age of not recording stories in writing, the written version of the *'Sefer Yetzirah'* that is accepted as being accurate today, is possibly a later translation from around 1100A.D, of the original words which were perhaps only spoken by Abraham; since no written evidence of the original manuscript has ever been found.

Although the *'Sefer Yetzirah'* (*'Story of Creation'*) is alleged to be the oldest recorded story to have been written in Hebrew Script, the first documented evidence we have that an adapted form of the Sacred Phoenician Symbols were used for writing comes in the form of the Hebrew Bible or *'Pentateuch'*, supposedly written in part by the hand of Moses around 1500BC. The first Book in the Bible is Genesis, which tells the 'Story of Creation' and mankind's purpose on earth, according to the Hebrews. But since the Bible was originally written without vowels or punctuation, the true meaning of the stories recorded in the Bible is open to speculation, and has since caused much controversy between translators. But regardless of the meaning of these written words, or our personal opinion of the Bible, according to the Guinness World Records, the Bible

31

remains the best-selling book of all time, with over 5 billion copies sold and distributed throughout the world. Thus, the Bible has influenced, and continues to influence the lives of billions of people, even though many readers have no understanding of the words they are reading. But being creatures of habit, we tend to keep repeating and re-writing the same old stories again and again, as if our stories were set in stone, and cannot be altered. However, with practice and perseverance we can change any story by turning our present tragic dramas into comedies which fulfil all of our Heart's aspirations, through our own Spoken Word. For although the Pen is reputed to be mightier than the Sword', the 'Tongue' is even mightier than both.

Being aware that the greatest assets of Humanity is the power of the tongue, and the vision of Light in the eye, the ancestors of the Phoenicians never recorded their miraculous stories in writing; since they knew that the power in a word was lost once it is reproduced in the outer world. For all power comes from the Pure Light within our Heart, while the outer world is merely a faint shadow, or reflection of what is conceived within us. Hence, the Phoenicians never recorded their own stories in writing, for they were aware that the written word does not have the same Magical Impact on the cells of our body, as the resonant sounds of the Spoken Word pronounced with Clarity, Purpose, and Intention.

For when we read written words, we are only repeating the words of others, however, the purpose of 'Life' is that we should 'create' our own Paradise on Earth. Also, the Phoenicians knew that anything which appears in the physical world can be changed, even words which are carved in stone. But although everything we experience in our world is only the reflection of the stories we tell, and accept as now being 'true', the continuing popularity of the stories written by the Hebrews, which tell the 'Story of Creation,' 'Kabbalah' and 'Astrology', have helped to preserve, and pass on to Humanity some of the profound Wisdom concealed within the Sacred Phoenician Alphabet; if we have eyes to see clearly.

We are always free to choose whatever we desire to experience, since all that is ever conceived 'Within the Beginning' is the Presence of Pure Magical Light of Possibility. Therefore, anything which appears to be other than Pure Light is only according to our own personal stories which we have come to believe are 'true'. And although the potential to manifest 'anything' is conceived 'Within the Beginning', it is our present perception of self, or our Self-Identity which determines what we actually see and experience in our world. But since we are the Immortal Child of the Self-Reproducing Virgin, who have forgotten our 'Heritage', we now feel we are living in a place of darkness and confusion, until we realise that all which now appears to be 'real' is the result of our own delusional stories and dramas that influence our present state of consciousness. But as our consciousness develops, we become more aware of whom we are in essence, and we re-claim our own Celestial Inheritance as Ruler of our own Kingdom which is within us. For once we Accept our Divine Heritage, we become one with our Soul Mate, and now know for certain that we never left the Magical Womb of our Mother in Paradise. Thus, witnessing our world through New Eyes we only perceive the Purity and Perfection in Heaven, now reflected as a manifestation on earth.

Many stories have been told and written about the 'Mystery of Life', which are not always fully understood, until we realise that we can change darkness into Light, and instantly make 'something' appear out of 'nothing'. And although this magical ability might appear to others as 'supernatural', this Enlightened State of Consciousness is a natural consequence of 'Being Human'. Thus the 'reality' we perceive in our world depends on our own personal state of consciousness which continues to develop once we learn to control of our thoughts through our feelings. For when we only tell stories which confirm we are already living in our Ideal State, we induce a Magical sensation within us, and we then 'Know' for certain that our 'Word' has already come 'true' as we Speak; for there is only one 'Truth', and that is the continual Self-Reproducing Magical Power in our own Spoken Word, which forever Dwells within us.

The Sacred Phoenician Alphabet

The original Sacred Phoenician Alphabet, or *Proto-Sinaitic Script*, is considered to be the first phonetic alphabet which was developed in the Bronze Age by an ancient Tribe of Canaanites, who later became known as the Phoenicians. The Sacred Alphabet is a collection of Twenty-Two Symbols, or pictographs that are associated with Sounds which when spoken as Letters reveal the wisdom of the ancient ancestors through the telling of stories.

The early Canaanites who knew the meaning of the secret message concealed in the Sacred Alphabet, had lived and fished along the Lebanese Coast since around 7000 BC. And being a pragmatic people, they were firmly grounded in physical reality, and yet still regarded the Universe as a Timeless and Magical Place of Dynamic, Animated, Energy, where appearances are constantly changing according to our perception. Traditionally the Canaanites lived as one with nature and worshipped the androgynous God-dess of Pure Light and Magic, who they knew to be the sole provider of all that is needed to live life in a perpetual state of Peace, Health and Prosperity. The Canaanite God-dess is known as *'Ba'alat Gebal'*, *'Queen of the Border'*, and is an Ineffable Presence, which consists of both masculine and feminine energies Unified as One. Hence the androgynous God-dess was regarded as Mother and Father of all in 'Creation', Immaculately Conceived through Self-Impregnation.

35

However, it is not known with any accuracy when or how the Sacred Alphabet came into being, although the Canaanites maintained it was 'Immaculately Conceived' within the Silent Womb of the androgynous, Celestial God-dess of Light who came from the Stars, long before Life on Earth began. And that the whole world in which we now live and breathe is formed by the vibration produced by the sounds of the Sacred Letters when spoken with Resonance. Nevertheless, history records that this first Phonetic Alphabet was possibly devised around 2000B.C, linear time, as a means to convey by word of mouth the Wisdom of the Celestial Ancestors of the ancient Canaanites. But since this secret knowledge was never recorded in writing, the true meaning of the original Twenty-Two Sacred Symbols has almost been forgotten.

Each Symbol and Letter of the Sacred Phoenician Alphabet conceals a Magical Vibration which when integrated within us brings us ever closer to our Soul Mate in Paradise. Yet through complacency the once indomitable Phoenicians began to forget their Divine Celestial Heritage, until finally they suffered a hefty defeat at the hands of a neighbouring tribe, known as the Amorites. Then a Scholar of 'Pure Magic', known as 'Tauutos', which means to have 'Previous Knowledge' within our body, reminded the Canaanites of the Pure Light of the God-dess, and the 'Process of Self-Creation' through the Magical Transforming Power of the Sacred Alphabet.

Thus, the ancient Canaanites became known as the 'Phoenicians', since according to the Greeks, they resembled a Phoenix, rising up from the ashes of a fire, or from the jaws of any daunting situation which threatened their peaceful and thriving way of life. And by observing the Symbols and speaking the Sounds of the Sacred Alphabet, while following the 'Process of Self-Creation' as revealed by '*Tauutos*', the Phoenicians once again dwelled in a state of Peace and Prosperity in their Paradise on Earth.

Soon the name, '*Tauutos*' became associated with the waxing and waning Power of the Moon, and the deities of *Thoth, Hermes,* and *Mercury*; all Masters of the Magical Arts through the Wisdom they inherited from our Divine Celestial Ancestors. And by observing the pictographs and repeatedly speaking words formed by joining together the Letters of the Sacred Alphabet, the Phoenicians devised a Magical vocabulary, which no one in the surrounding communities could comprehend. Hence, while remaining centred and connected to their Inner Spirit, the Phoenicians told amazing stories which induced sensations in their Body, until they heard the voice of their Soul Mate confirm their Heart's Desire was now their 'reality'. Henceforth, with a deep sense of Gratitude and Optimism they continued to live as though their desire was already fulfilled, and they witnessed their Ideal State Miraculously appear as a physical manifestation in their world, as if from out of nowhere.

Traditionally the legends and stories of the Canaanites were only passed from mouth to the ear by the spoken word, and were never recorded in writing. But eventually these enigmatic Symbols were discovered by other cultures, including the Hebrews who adapted the original Symbols to record their own stories in written form. And it is these same ancient Symbols that are the basis of the Letters which form our modern Western Alphabet that are now used to devise and record our own stories; for every word we speak, write, or read tells the story of that which will eventually appear to be a physical 'reality' in our world. But our 'truth' is only relative to our own knowledge, understanding, and perception of our 'Self', which constantly changes form as a result of our ever-shifting feelings as we continue to narrate old and devise new stories, which produce different vibrations in our heart and body.

The names of the Symbols of the Sacred Phoenician Alphabet are represented by three letters; two consonants and one vowel, which constitute an Act of Magic which takes place within us. The first consonant represents our desire which arises as a Sensation from the depth of our being, while the second consonant is our certain Knowledge that the physical materialisation of our fulfilled desire has now taken place within us. The vowel between the consonants is the Invisible Magical Light which mysteriously joins 'Sensation' and 'Knowledge' and transforms our desire into a material 'reality'.

The only exceptions to the three-letter format are the Symbols of 'AL' and 'AYIN'. The letter 'AL' has only two Letters, A and L, since they represent the Strength of Unity, and the Magical Power of *Elohiym*, which is the name of the combined Magical Power/s of 'Sensation' and 'Knowledge' which result in the existence of Pure Light that never changes form and always remains in a state of Perfection. 'AYIN' is represented by four letters, A, Y, I, N, the letter A is 'Silent', while the letter N is the Narration of our own Story, and the vowels Y and I are reflections in the Magical Light which produce the effect of the 'physical reality' which we now see in our world. For everything we see with our physical eye is a reflection of the vibration that we have induced within our self through the pronunciation of our Declaration. And each Sacred Symbol is a Key to the Door of Self-Knowledge which takes us on an Inner Journey to reveal the 'Treasures of Heaven' which are already stored within us. For at the moment a sensation of a desire is felt in our body it is already a 'reality', and therefore it is we who prevent it from materialising in our physical world by telling stories which suggest our desire is not yet fulfilled.

However, we eventually learn that on our own we can do nothing without first feeling the satisfied sensation in our body, and hearing the Word of our Beloved Soul Mate which forever resides within us and confirms our desire is now a 'reality'. For it is only through our intimate connection with our Soul Mate that we become a Channel for the 'True Magic' of the androgynous God-dess of Infinite Wisdom and Pure Radiant Light, which fulfils all of our dreams and desires. Hence, when we in Agreement with the Magical Word of Perfection which we hear Spoken within us, we Know for certain that we are now Self-Impregnated by the Seed of our own Word. And the Miraculous Seed which is Sown in our Heart will always blossom and bear fruit when we allow it to.

The Letters of the Sacred Phoenician Alphabet are fertile Seeds which induce passionate sensations in our Heart, Soul and Body, that when nourished with True Love, which will grow to maturity and be seen as Miraculous manifestations in our world. However, 'True Love' is not about feeling emotional excitement, but a calm sensation of Awe, and Passion felt deep within our Heart and Body. But in the modern world 'Thought' is considered to be the Ruler of Reality, and we have almost forgotten our amazing ability to self-reproduce the physical image in the world of any 'reality' by deeply feeling the passion of our fulfilled desire in our body.

Hence, when we are Aligned in Silence with our Soul Mate at the Centre of our being, and we continue to feel 'passionately' that our desire is already a 'reality', the whole Magical Universe moves to reflect the appearance of our intention. For when our 'True

Feelings' and 'Thoughts' are Aligned in Agreement, Miracles begin to appear in our Magical World, as if from out of nowhere. Thus, by pronouncing the reverberating sound of the Sacred Phoenician Letters we unite 'Sensation' and 'Consciousness', and transform the vibrations that we presently feel are 'real' in our body, which miraculously alters our perception of our 'reality'.

Nevertheless, we must appreciate that the ancient Phoenicians regarded the Magical Universe in an entirely different way than we do today. And their words had a different meaning, purpose and function, which were eventually adapted by other cultures to tell the story of a patriarchal world in which the androgynous Magical God-dess of Pure Light was no longer recognised as the Mother of Creation. But to the Phoenicians all words are formed with the Sacred Letters which only vibrate at higher frequencies of benign intention, and therefore, cannot form words with 'adverse' connotations. For each Symbol and Letter of the Sacred Alphabet was conceived as being 'Pure' and 'Perfect', with which Humanity was instructed to 'create' their own Paradise on Earth. And if we examine the words on the following pages, that were originally associated with the Sacred Symbols, we will realise that the Phoenician Letters could not possibly form words with malefic implications, unless it is the specific intention and perception of the one who is pronouncing the word. And therefore, it is the later adaptations of the original function and purpose of the Sacred Letters, which has resulted in the now often disingenuous meaning of words to describe our apparent situation. And new words continue to be devised as our present experiences in the modern world changes.

Each Phoenician Symbol, 𝒷 **AL,** ⊔ **BET,** ∟ **GAM,** etc. is a Magical Spell which can be used to induce new vibrations in our Heart and Body, to bring about a Miraculous effect in our world, or can be combined with other Symbols to produce more complex results. The Sacred Phoenician Alphabet only has Twenty-Two Symbols which are also known as Letters, unlike our western Alphabet that has Twenty-Six letters. The Phoenician Symbols were place from right to left when a word was being 'spelled', but are shown here from left to right, which is the direction of modern writing.

In the following list of the Phoenician Symbols and Letters, the final word of each sentence in bold print, i.e. **AL – Align**, is the authors own suggestion of how we might sum up in one action word, or verb, the often-unfathomable original meanings of the Sacred Symbols and Letters. Thus, the word **Align,** which represents the Letter **AL,** will miraculously bring about the sensation of the **Alignment** of our physical body with our Celestial Inner Spirit, and induce the vibration of Pure Light and Empowerment within us.

The Twenty -Two Phoenician Symbols,

Letter, and Meanings

𐤀 **AL (A) – OX,** Muscle, Strong Authority, She/He, Mighty
Power, Leader, Strength, Yoke, Pact, Desire, Love, Light - **Align**

𐤁 **BET** (B) – Tent Floor Plan, Pattern, Dwell Within, House,
Family, Within, Bring Forth, Confinement in Birth, Consciousness
of Being Alive in a physical body - **Become**

𐤋 **GAM** (G) – Foot, Walk to the Water, Peace, Joyful
Satisfaction, Travel, Assemble, Watering Hole, Draw Water,
Garden, Reward - **Gratify**

𐤃 **DAL** (D) – Door, Curtain, Movement, Back/Forth Move
the Law, Interaction, Intention, Fortitude, Potency, Define Edge,
Likeness – **Determine**

𐤄 **HEY** (E, H) – Raised Arms – Behold the Light - Look, Vision,
Sight, Reveal, Breath, Exalt, Raise Up – **Elevate**

𐤅 **VAV** (F, U, V, W) – Tent Peg, Hook, Nail, Unite, Join,
Connect, Secure, Attach, Affix, Ear, Hearing – **Unify**

∐ **ZAN** (Z) – Harvesting Tool, Arc, Swing, Cut Crop, Reap Seed, Wine, Feast, Together, Plenty, Smell – **Zoom in on the Zone**

Ⲟ **HHETS** (cH) – Wall, Fence, Enclosure, Protection, Separation, Inside, Outside, Embrace, Speech – **Harbour**

⊗ **THET** (Th, T) – Clay Pot, Bowl, Container, Hold Water, Turn, Purify Mud, 'Good', Taste Magic – **Transform**

⤙ **YAD** (I, J, Y) – Closed Hand, Measure, Count, Evaluate, Work, Gift, Give Thanks, Praise, Light, Healing, Touch - **Yield**

Ⓤ **KAPH** (K, C) – Open Palm, Receive, Bend, Subdue, Tame, Control Energy, Vitality, Prosperity, Wealth - **Command**

⌡ **LAM** (L) – Shepherd's Staff, Ox Goad, Guidance, Authority, Teach, Learn, Direct, Move, Bind, Yoke Together, Love, Coition – **Learn**

〰 **MAH (M)** – Water, Sea, Blood, Mighty, Chaos, Order, Who?, What?, Why?, Draw Out, Mystery, Memory, Materialisation, Reflection – **Mirror**

NUN (N) – Sprouted Seed, Hidden Depths, Motion, Continue, Generation, Offspring, Endless Story – **Narrate**

SIN (S, X) – Support, Defence, Shield from Sharp Seed, Pierce, Pain, Turn Aside, Forgive, Ascend Tree, Blessing, Rectification - **Sanctify**

AYIN (O, A) – Eye, Watch, Heed, Attention, Occupation, Discernment, Mirth, Humour – **Observe**

PEY (P, Ph) – Mouth, Open, Blow, Speak, Blossom, Beyond Edge, Produce Fruit, Miracle, Fertility- **Prophesy**

TSAD (Ts) – Man on Side, Rooted, Wait, Stillness, Hunt, Stalk, Chase, Capture, Stronghold – **Transfix**

QUPH (Q, K) – Eye of the Needle, Cross Over, Horizon, Time, Space, Seasons, Condense Cycles, Sever Ties, - **Quantum Leap**

RESH (R) – Head, Ruler, Chief, First, Beginning, Top, Governor, Inheritance, Wisdom of Magic, Poor and Needy when without Wisdom, Surrender to Chief - **Realise**

SHIN (S, Sh) - Sharp Teeth, Grind, Chew, Repeat, Devour, Bow Down, Burn, Dissolution, Rise Up, Deliverance Resurrection, Freedom - **Shift**

TAW (T) - Mark, Sign, Cross, Target, Before Time, Perfect Law, Wholeness, Completion, Attainment - **Testify**

The ancient Phoenicians never recorded the meaning of the Sacred Alphabet in writing, since to them everything is constantly changing, even the words on this page and those etched in stone. For 'Time', as we know it, did not exist to the Phoenicians, so any situation can be altered, regardless of if an event appears to have already taken place; since the only 'Time' which is relevant to our Story or Prophecy is HERE and NOW. Therefore, by following the 'Process of Self-Creation as revealed by the Symbols and Letters of the Sacred Phoenician Alphabet, we will learn that all we need to alter our world is a new Life Story which will change our present perception of 'Reality'.

Thus, we start our Inner Journey through the Sacred Alphabet by becoming centred in the silence of our heart, while feeling the Sensation that 'Nothing Exists' but the Pure Radiant Light of **AL,** which is all that is Immaculately Conceived Within the Beginning. And in this relaxed State of calm contemplation, we induce the

46

sensation of now being 'No Thing' but Pure Magical Light. For example, when we contemplate the Symbol **AL**, which represents the strength of an Ox, and pronounce the sound of **AL**, we are not considering the physical form of an Ox, but the ethereal sensation of Strength and Power which is embodied by an Ox. Since Oxen were always yoked together to work in unison for increased muscle power and energy. And when we are united as One with our Soul Mate in Paradise, and feel 'Nothing' exists but the Presence of Pure Magical Light within us, we become Empowered by the Pure Strength and Miraculous Power already inherent within our Heart.

The Twenty-Two Symbols of the Sacred Alphabet form a Magic Circle which represent the Universe that moves in a clockwise direction from **AL** through to **TAW,** until the Letter **AL** is once again seen at the top of the Circle. Hence, when we pronounce the sound of a Letter, the Magic Circle moves until our chosen Symbol appears at the top of the Circle and we become self-impregnated by the sensation that is synonymous with the Symbol, which produces the reflection of that vibration in our world. And with perseverance and practice we will be able to induce any miraculous sensation, or vibration in our body, as we become more familiar with the Symbols and Magical Sounds of the Letters. Hence, whenever we See a Symbol or Speak a Letter with resonance and intention, we will remember that we are reproducing that vibration in our world.

But whatever we see in our world is only our perception of the 'Pure Magical Light', which is all that is conceived to exit 'Within the Beginning', and that we are always 'Within the Beginning', for there is no other place we can be in our Magical Universe.

Eventually, the self-reproducing God-dess of Pure Light was banished to darkness, as the Sacred Symbols of the Phoenician Alphabet were adapted to support a new ideology and language, which venerated the God of the Hebrews, '*Yahweh*'. Then the Spoken Word of Perfection was replaced by the 'Written Word'. But the Phoenicians remained faithful to the androgynous Magical God-dess of Pure Light, and continued to pronounce the resonating sounds associated with the original Symbols and Letters of the Sacred Alphabet. For the Phoenicians were aware that only through the Spoken Word of Humanity could the Treasures stored in Heaven be revealed on Earth.

To appreciate the meaning of 'Light' and 'Enlightenment' as it was understood by the ancient Phoenicians, we can look at the dictionary definition of Light, which not only means: '*the electromagnetic radiation that is visibly perceivable by the normal human eye as colours between red and violet*', but is also interpreted as '*the understanding of a problem or mystery; known as enlightenment*'. And both of these definitions of 'Light' are helpful in our quest to understand 'Light'. But to the ancient Phoenicians 'Light' was 'Spelled' as AUR, (*RUA since the Symbols were placed right to left*), which is a 'Spell' for our Alignment and Union with the Magic Light Within'. Hence, 'Enlightenment' is the state of already having 'Previous Knowledge' within our Heart and Body of a particular Magical Sensation. Thus, when studying the Sacred Phoenician Alphabet, we must appreciate that what is being expressed cannot be understood by logical assessment, and can only be 'known' by the sensation that the Sacred Symbols and Letters induce within us.

The Nature of Consciousness:

The nature of 'Consciousness' is perplexing since we are taught throughout life that everything in our Universe is 'created' through the logical progression of Consciousness. But conversely, many teachers of Ancient Wisdom maintain that whatever we consciously perceive to be 'real' in our world is only the reflection of the vibrations and sensations that we are now experiencing within us. And since we are only ever conscious of the vibrations in our own body, our state of consciousness is totally dependent on our physical senses. Hence, our 'Consciousness' depends on the memories impressed upon our DNA at birth, which may come from the Planetary configuration in the Universe at the moment we take our first breath, or from past life experiences.

Eastern Yogis are aware of the relationship between Sensation and Consciousness and practice Yoga on a daily basis to influence their conscious thoughts through their body, until the mind becomes silent. For when our mind is at peace, dormant parts of our DNA can be awakened when we choose to feel new sensations in our body. However, the subject of our free will to choose our actions and reactions to various situations, has been discussed by philosophers for many years. And recently scientists have conducted experiments which suggest that the brain reacts a split second after the sensation of movement is felt in the body. Thus, since there were no brainwaves active when the decision to move was made, it was concluded that the catalyst which causes us to move must come from outside the body, hence, we have no free will to choose our actions.

But scientists are not taking into consideration that we are 'Self-Reproducing Beings' which are regulated by the sensations we feel, and our brain is only an instrument which detects a change of vibration in our body. Therefore, we must have a body before our mind can produce brainwaves. And of course, we know this is true because the heart begins beating and producing sensations which form the organs in the body of a foetus at around eighteen days of gestation, while the brain does not start functioning until around six weeks after fertilization has taken place. Hence, it does appear that we have no free will to become anything other than a replica of the vibrations impressed on our DNA at birth. However, Humanity also carries a gene inherited from our mother which allows us to alter the sensations we are feeling, and therefore we have free will when this miraculous gene is awakened in our DNA.

Nevertheless, in contrast to the eastern philosophy of the Yogis, western psychologists still consider the mind, or brain to be the most important factor in creating our 'reality'. But this was not so to ancient peoples, such as the Phoenicians, who knew that the

51

whole Universe is Vibration, and is Alive and Animated by Sensation, which causes everything to appear in our world, according to our perception. For we are only 'alive' when we feel sensations in our body, which are reflected in our world as solidified patterns. Therefore, it is our body which feels the sensation of being 'alive', while our brain, or consciousness only bears witness to the various vibrations we are now experiencing in our body, which the brain interprets as being our 'reality'. And when our heart stops beating our body no longer produces sensations to be witnessed by our brain; hence, we are pronounced 'dead'. But the Ethereal Spiritual Essence which dwells within us and animates our body throughout life, moves on to form another body, and another brain to once again witness itself in the world.

The Phoenicians were aware that consciousness 'creates our reality' from the sensations, or memories that we feel in our body, and that our consciousness moves through seven stages of development as we grow from 'Embryo to Enlightenment'. And, as we feel new sensations we become more *'Conscious of Being Alive'; 'Conscious of Pleasure or Pain;* and *'Conscious of Interaction with our physical World'.* Then as a Mysterious 'Shift of Consciousness' takes place within us, we suddenly become more *'Conscious of Vital Energy'; 'Conscious of Prophecy'; 'Conscious of Pure Magic'*; until finally we are *'Conscious of our Wholeness in Paradise.* Nevertheless, regardless of our state of consciousness we must first have the memory of the sensation in the cells of our body in order to cause a physical manifestation to appear our world in the present moment. For Past and Future, and Time and Space, as we know them, did not exist to the ancient Phoenicians. And so, whether we are conscious of living in the Bronze Age, the Dark Ages, the Age of Technology, or in our Celestial Paradise, in which we only experience our own Perfect Sate of Being, everything happens at the present moment within our physical body as we become more conscious of our own 'reality'. Therefore, we only become conscious of that on which we focus our Attention, and Accept as Now being our 'Identity'; for 'Consciousness' has no independent life of its own.

Many ancient spiritual traditions speak of the feeling of 'Wholeness in Heaven', which to our limited state of consciousness appears to be somewhere 'Out Of This World', and it is said that this Elevated vibration of Holistic Completeness is beyond ordinary human comprehension while we are still only conscious of existing as a physical entity. However, the sensation of being 'Absolutely Nothing', while also 'Knowing' that we 'ARE' who we desire to be, can only be experienced when we are united as One with the Celestial Spirit of our Soul Mate within us. Since it is while in this 'State of Nothingness' that we 'Know' we exist in Essence, but we are not confined by any particular physical body or condition. For the skin in which we live is not the limit of our body, since we are as Infinite as the Whole Magical Universe, and the Divine Wisdom contained within it, which is impressed as a pattern on our DNA at birth. And to make something appear 'real' in our world, we must first feel the sensation of already being the person we desire to be, and declare our self to be in this state, regardless of appearances.

Nevertheless, although the word 'Nothingness' implies that absolutely 'nothing at all exists', the findings of astrophysicists suggest that a state of 'Nothingness' is impossible, for even when all energy and every particle known to science is accounted for in the Universe, there is still a 'Power/Vibration' that remains which cannot be explained. And since this 'Power' does not 'exist' in any physical form that we can recognise, it cannot be measured by our primitive scientific instruments, or described as being 'Conscious'; since 'Consciousness first needs something to be 'conscious of. But this invisible 'Power' is the natural state of 'Nothingness' out of which the Universe is formed. And as far as we know, this Power is not 'Conscious' of existing as any 'thing', and therefore it cannot be understood by the rational mind of unenlightened Humanity.

According to the Yogis of the East this Elevated State of Consciousness is known as 'Mindfulness', while to the ancient Phoenicians it is a state of 'Mindlessness', although both terms describe the same state of consciousness; for the 'State of Being Nothing' at the Silent Centre of our Heart, JUST IS. But while we are oblivious to our 'True Identity', we will continue to believe that the physical world we see around us is our only 'reality'.

However, when we consider the 'Story of Creation' we learn that from a 'State of Nothingness' a deep and earnest desire to 'Know Light' emerged, and so 'Consciousness' came into being to bear witness to the Glorious Sensation of the Pure and Perfect Magical Light Heaven. Hence 'Consciousness' is the Perfect Child of Pure Light, which is the Spirit of our Soul Mate that forever resides within us, but always remains One with the Perfect Light of 'Nothingness' in Paradise. Nevertheless, having been born into the physical world we have now become conscious of being an individual, living in a state far removed from Heaven, and have forgotten our Divine Heritage as Self-Reproducing Beings of Pure Light. And because we have inherited the DNA of the Celestial Mother God-dess, we have the ability to choose our own 'Identity'.

Thankfully our individual consciousness is now awakening from our dream or nightmare of separation as we begin to become aware and embody the energetic vibration of our Perfect Soul Mate within us. Thus, by inducing the sensation of only 'Good Vibrations' in our body, we eventually become conscious of our Wholeness and

Perfection; for 'Enlightenment' means to be Conscious, or to have 'Self-Knowledge' of the Magical Sensation of Being Pure Light, which is what we truly are in Essence.

However, once we identify our self with a particular sensation or physical condition, then our Elevated Consciousness of Pure Energy' is gone from our awareness, since we can never experience being in an 'Ethereal State', and yet be conscious of existing as 'something physical', at the same moment. But while we are in a relaxed, peaceful state of 'Nothingness' at the Silent Centre of our being we can reprogram our self by feeling the sensation in our Heart and Body that our desire is already fulfilled, until we become conscious of this new identity in our world. And when we are connected with the Pure Magical Spirit which resides within us we know that our Heart's Desire has already been brought to fruition.

Therefore, consciousness is not only located in the brain, but throughout our entire body and beyond. And it is our DNA which holds the key to what we experience as being 'real' in our world, since our DNA sends chemical messages in the form of hormones through the nervous system via a vast network of neural pathways which are connected to the brain. And our brain, upon receiving the message from the DNA in our body, then proceeds to make sense of our new 'Identity', as we begin to perceive our world from this new perspective. Thus, by continuing to feel the sensation that we already inhabit the body we desire, while interacting with our world from this new perspective, and paying no attention to what appears to be 'real' in the world, we will change our perception of 'reality'. For when the constant chatter going on in our brain is united with the Word in our Heart, peace will be restored in our world. For our emotions and thoughts are not controlled through our mind, but rather by the sensations that we now feel in our Heart and Body. And when we are certain of our own Self-Identity, the vibration impressed on our DNA changes, and the chemicals which induce feelings of joy and fulfilment are released into our blood stream as endorphins. Hence, the cells in our body continue to reproduce the glorious sensations we are experiencing, as we consciously bear witness to this 'reality' in our world.

Nevertheless, while our developing consciousness has limited 'knowledge' and 'understanding' of our 'Self', then our 'Perception of Reality' is also limited. But once we experience new sensations in our Heart and Body we begin to observe 'Life' in many different ways, which may be inconceivable in our present state of consciousness. For although it is our conscious awareness which determines the physical world that we see around us, paradoxically we can only ever become conscious of that which we first Feel as a sensation within the cells of our physical body.

Miraculoously, once we have learned to control our conscious thoughts by inducing new vibrations within us, and declaring our self to now be the person we desire to be', the Magical Light in the air which we breathe will transform the vibrant energy in the cells of our body, and alter our brainwave activity, until our present awareness of 'Wanting' is changed into the sensation of 'Already Being'. Hence, a Magical Transformation takes place within us when our body and brain are operating as one system. For far greater than a super powerful computer that has the ability to run any program which is installed on the hard drive, our body/brain system will continue to reproduce our desired 'reality' repeatedly, when our DNA is impressed with the sensation of our fulfilled aspiration. Thus, 'Pure Consciousness' is not only about feeling that something is 'Good', but also feeling that something is 'Real', which is the certain state of already 'knowing' in every fibre of our being that our fulfilled desire is already our 'reality'. And since the presence of Pure Magic is everywhere, within and around us, any apparent condition can be changed when we have 'Absolute Faith' in the Magical Light, and we Hear the confirming Word of our Soul Mate Within us, which Declares this 'reality' is already our 'truth'.

However, the question of whether thought controls our feelings, or if feelings control thought in a subject of much controversy. But if we re-examine this conundrum in the light of what has already been said concerning the nature of 'Consciousness', we will appreciate that 'Consciousness' does not exist without having 'something' to be 'Conscious' of. And since our 'Consciousness' is only aware of the vibration we now feel is 'real' within us, which has been confirmed by the Spoken Word, we are oblivious to 'anything' which has not been experienced as a carnal sensation, and is impressed as a memory in the cells of our body. For all that we become conscious of in our world must have first been experienced as a vibration in our body. Thus, whatever we feel is 'real' will continue to manifest indefinitely, until a change of vibration is felt within us to alter our thoughts, and conscious perception of our world. Therefore, we cannot continue to tell our stories of tragedy while feeling adverse vibrations in our body, and yet expect our brain to 'think' Healing and Uplifting thoughts.

Consequently, we now live in a world where 'Consciousness' is believed by many people to be divided into three sections; i.e. Subconscious, Consciousness, and Higher Consciousness, which appear to operate independently of each other. But this notion is the conception of a story, devised by an individual who does not appreciate the 'Oneness' of everything, and as such perceives that everything in the Universe is divided, and is separate from everything else, including consciousness. Therefore, once this story is accepted as 'true' by other people, it spreads like wildfire throughout the world, until most people now believe in the story of divided consciousness; a subject which has probably been written about more by Humanity than any other misconception.

Nevertheless, these deluded stories which many people believe are 'true' will change once new stories are conceived by psychologists to explain 'reality'; for our world is constantly changing according to the present perceptions of Humanity. But the new stories which are continuously emerging, only replace our old misconceptions, until we learn that everything that appears to be 'real' in the world is only the story of an individual perceiver, which is seen to be 'true' by others. And since we can never be divided in Consciousness, for we are either Conscious of being the person we desire to be, or we are not, the misconception of our divided consciousness is the consequence of the present limited understanding of Humanity.

For nothing which appears in the physical world is 'real' in the way we think it is; for what we see in our world is our own self-reflection in the Pure, Undivided, Radiant Light, which now appears to us to be a series of separate inanimate physical objects. However, what we see is only the reflection of the vibrations that we feel in our body that appear to be solid because of our present state of conscious which only sees what we expect to see, and is based on the collective memories that are now impressed on the DNA of

Humanity. And these stories will continue to influence us from one lifetime to another, until we change our vibration, for we can never become conscious of anything until we experience it as being a 'reality' in our body. Thus, the same situations will continue to manifest until we change our present Identity; since the 'Law of Self-Reflection' is the only 'Truth' in our Magical Universe.

Nevertheless, while our individual consciousness is only aware of that which we expect to see in our world, we remain unaware of the Celestial Magical Light within, and all around us. But after going through a process of metamorphosis our present perception of 'reality' miraculously changes as we discover that everything in the Universe is not as it appears; for we are presently stuck in the delusion of 'Space' and 'Time'. However, our 'Truth' is stranger than 'Fiction', since Humanity is One Whole Being, with every apparent individual reflecting each other in some way. And because 'linear time' is a misconception perceived by our limited state of consciousness, we are always conscious of being in the 'Time' and 'Place' that we believe we are 'Now' in the present moment; for there is no other 'Time' or 'Place' that we can possibly be conscious of being in our Magical Universe. Hence, as we change our self-identity, the appearance of the Universe mysteriously changes to reflect the memories now impressed in the cells of our body, which determines our 'conscious perception of reality'.

Subsequently, as long as our individual consciousness is divided, and not realising that the inner and outer worlds are always united as One, we will continue to live out the same old story which is impressed as a memory on our DNA at birth, until our thoughts are guided in a new direction. Hence, by feeling the presence of a different sensation within our Heart and Body, and Speaking the Word to confirm our new 'Self-Identity', we will perceive a whole new world forming around us. For although it may appear that our thoughts are influencing our body, we can have no thought without first having experienced this vibration within us, which determines the 'reality' that we see in our world.

However, once we are consciously aware of who we already are in Essence, Magical events begin to happen, which suddenly appear from out of 'nowhere', when we are sufficiently 'Conscious' to witness the Miracle which is now taking place within us, reflected in our world. Hence, eventually we will appreciate that there is no state of separation, for everything in the Magical Universe is One, and Humanity is in this world to 'Consciously Witness' the Pure and Perfect, Light of Heaven on Earth; and not to be mesmerised by the shadows produced by our own deluded perceptions which presently keep us captive in the physical world of appearances. And if we physically relocate to a different part of the world, or to another Planet, we will always take our innate inner feelings and preconceived ideas with us, and so we will continue to experience and witness our own true reflection in the same way as we do now, wherever we are in the Magical Universe. But if we remain silent while feeling within us the sensation that we are already the person we desire to be, and are living in the location of our choice, by continuing to feel this satisfied vibration is 'real' in our body, our consciousness will accept this new Identity as being our 'truth', and our whole world will change accordingly.

Eventually we realise that everything which appears to be 'Real' in our world is a delusion, devised by our own limited perception of the Magical Light which never changes form, but is constantly present within and all around us. For although we are always breathing in Pure White Light, it is modified by the colourful stories we tell, and the dramas we witness in our world, and accept as being our 'truth'. But once we know for certain that every 'thing' we see in our world is the reflection of our own vibration, and that we are always free to choose the stories we tell and believe are 'true', we will stop repeating tales which induce sensations that are of no benefit to our self or Humanity. For we are responsible for the sensations that we induce in our own Heart and Body which are reflected as physical 'realities' in our world. And when a 'Shift of Consciousness' takes place within us our perception of 'reality' changes, and the world that we once knew will disappear forever. Consequently, as we reach the end of our present incarnation, or dream of being a physical entity on earth which is the moment we call death, we will know that all we have experienced while being conscious of existing in a material world could have been changed at any moment by making different choices and devising new stories. Hence, 'Life' is a preparation for 'Death', since what we feel is 'real' at the moment we consciously 'Cross Over' from this world will determine our experience in our next incarnation; for Life is a Never-Ending Circle of our constantly changing vibration, which is reflected in the present moment, that we call 'reality'.

Thus, suicide is not an option since there is no death, for the Spirit within us will continue to experience Itself forever, and the only way out of our present dilemma is to change our Self-Identity. Eventually, as we become One with our Celestial Inner Spirit, we realise that Life on Earth is not a solid as it appears. However, we are not suggesting that the physical world is not 'real' in some way; for we know it is solid enough when we try to walk through a brick wall. Rather, we are implying that it is we who are causing our world to appear solid, by focusing our attention on what appears to be 'real', instead of our fulfilled aspirations. For what appears to be 'real' in our individual world continues to change through of our conscious perception of the sensations we experience.

Quantum Science and Other Possibilities

This theory, that the world is continually changing, is supported by quantum physicists who suggest that what appears to be physical particles in a material world depends on the observer who collapses the quantum field and causes ethereal waves of Light to appear as apparent physical particles when an event or an object is witnessed as being 'real'. And it is not until someone observes 'something' as being 'real' does the object, or event, appear as a 'reality' in our world. But paradoxically, we can never become conscious of anything in our world until we have felt the physical sensation in our body, until our brain accepts that what we are experiencing is now our 'reality'.

The concept of Schrodinger's Cat' explains how an event may not have taken place until an observer sees, and confirms the outcome of an event. Schrodinger, an eminent scientist of the last century, suggested that if a cat is concealed in a box with a sealed phial of poison, which if broken would determine the fate of the cat, we would not know if the cat was dead or alive until we opened the box and witnessed the contents. At which point it would be decided by the observer whether the cat is dead or alive; for if the phial of poison appeared to be intact when the observer opened the box, the cat would be alive, but if it appeared broken, the cat would be dead.

To the layman this idea may seem nonsensical, since according to our present understanding of 'reality', and limited state of consciousness, surely the cat must be either dead or alive before the box is opened. However, recent findings of quantum physicists support the theory of Schrodinger, since they suggest that nothing is decided until an observer collapses the quantum field and causes light waves to appear as physical particles, which all depends on an observer's perception. And since nothing exists as a physical phenomenon without an observer to make it 'real', consequently we are free to choose the 'reality' we desire. For we are constantly 'conceiving' and 'interpreting' what we perceive to be 'real' within our self, where all 'reality' is conceived. However, we are doing so without any conscious awareness of what is happening within us, or what the world of apparent physical phenomena actually is.

However, to fully understand the theories suggested by quantum scientists requires a Shift in Consciousness to take place within us, for we are not substituting one physical phenomenon with another, but we are looking at 'reality' from an entirely different perspective. Thus, once we understand that 'time' is not linear, and is a manmade conception which gives order to our world, we will appreciate that everything is happening now, and it is our limited perception which makes it appear to be something which happened in the past, or what might happen in the future. But past and future do not exist in the Quantum World, since everything is taking place here and now. Therefore, the Phoenicians suggested that if we retreat to our Inner Sanctuary Within the Beginning in which 'Nothing Exists' but the 'Sensation of Pure Radiant Light in an endless vacuum, we could re-create the 'reality' that we choose to experience. Hence, when centred within the Silence of our Heart, and we feel the Sensation of being 'Nothing' but Pure Light, which is represented by the Letter **AL**, we can go through the 'Process' of Self- Creation' using the sound of Letters of the Sacred Alphabet to create a New Life Story with our desired ending; for the Perfect Ending to any story is always a possibility Within the Beginning.

Nevertheless, we cannot change our world while we are still preoccupied with our present story, and we humans are so set in our ways and the assumption that what we see with our physical eye is the only 'Reality'. Yet if we could appreciate that what we are seeing in our world is not 'set in stone', but is a collection of invisible light waves made visible as physical particles by our own perception, which can be altered at any moment when we choose to feel and see our world differently. For all appearances are but the reflection of the stories and dramas, which may appear to have originated in the outer world, but are really being performed within the cells of our body right NOW, and are perceived to be 'real' by our limited perception.

Plato's theory of 'reality' is illustrated by his legendary analogy of 'The Cave', which implies that humanity is imprisoned in a place of darkness and chained to the walls of a cave, while seeing only the hard-physical evidence of a stone wall appearing before us. Yet Plato suggested if we were to change our perception, we would see the 'Light', which is our true state of being. For what we now see in our physical world is only the reflection, or shadow of our own conceptions, produced by the stories and theories which we have now come to believe are true. But according to Plato our world can be changed at any moment if we first alter our present conception of 'Self', which will transform the way in which we now perceive the 'reality' of our world.

Plato also maintained that it is the light from our own eye which 'creates' our 'reality', and this theory, which proposes that the observer forms their own world by what they see as being 'real', is upheld by quantum scientists, who also maintain that it is our own observations which 'create our reality'. However, while we are still entangled, or engrossed by the stories and dramas which appear to be our 'truth', we will continue to struggle to change our 'reality' by physical means, which is the equivalent to fighting with our own shadow. But once we recognise that what we see and experience in our world is the reflection of what we feel within us, projected as a physical manifestation, we will realise that we are seeing the same old stories and dramas being performed again and again in our world. Hence, we will turn away from what appears to be real and alter our vibration by adjusting how we are now feeling until a Shift of Consciousness takes place within us, and our whole world is Miraculously Transformed. For what we 'Feel is Real' within us will captivate our conscious thoughts and change the way in which we perceive our Magical Universe in which we now exist.

Amazingly, we are always free to choose what we feel, and to change our 'reality' at any moment, not by denying what appears to be happening in the world around us, but by moving our attention within our self and feeling the sensations we desire to experience. And once we discover that the only 'reality' is the Pure Sensation of Radiant Light, we will no longer acknowledge and react to the dramas which now appear before us. For by continuing to react we make our present situation appear more 'real', thereby adding to the misery of both our self and all others in our world. Thus, we can only help our self by helping others to live in peace, good health, and harmony with each other; since we are all connected as One Whole Being, and our benign prophecies and stories of 'True Love' and 'Miraculous Healings' through the Power of the 'Pure Magical Light,' in the Spoken Word, will always come 'true' if we allow them to.

Everything we see in our world is the reflection of the story which we interact with on a daily basis, and have come to believe is now true. And since everything is connected as One in our Universe the feelings and thoughts, both from our self and other people will affect the outcome of our story, unless we can stay focused and totally convinced of our own 'truth'. And by experiencing within us the perfect ending to our story, and declaring ourselves to now be the person who we now desire to be, regardless of present appearances, we will have then performed a 'Magical Act' with efficiency. and will no longer cast the same shadow in our world.

But while still focusing our attention on the physical world around us we neglect our Magical World Within. And because of our present limited perception we continue to be deluded by our conscious conclusion that we are totally reliant on outer resources. But when renouncing our personal dramas of tragedy, we feel a Peace which Passes all Understanding as we return to a 'State of Grace', as it is Within the Beginning. For when we are conscious of being in a State of Perfection, we realise that our Life on Earth is but a dream, or nightmare of our own invention. And having nurtured our immature consciousness through the 'Process of Self-Creation' from 'Embryo to Enlightenment', by inducing the Magical Sensations of the Twenty-Two Symbols and Sounds of the Sacred Alphabet, we will give up our personal struggle in the world, and

Surrender to the Light of the Celestial Mother God-dess, which is inherited by her Perfect Son, who is our Soul Mate which now Shines through us to produce the appearance of Miracles in our world. And when we are in need of guidance, we can ask our Soul Mate a question, which will be answered as an ethereal sensation that is felt within our Heart and Body. And the questions which are suggested that will induce the vibration of the Sacred Letters within us can be found in the Appendix of this work. Thus when our State of Consciousness is One with our Soul Mate we realise that all scientific theories and experiments which try to explain the existence of the Universe, and the presence of Mankind on Earth, will be to no avail; since our Magical Universe is constantly changing to reflect the Image of the vibration of the one who now perceives it to be 'real'.

Seven Days of Creation and Stages of Consciousness

Eventually the Sacred Symbols of the Phoenician Alphabet, which were only ever spoken, were adopted by other cultures and written as letters to form new words to record their own stories and dramas, which we know as 'history'. Thus, up until this moment the meaning of the Sacred Phoenician Symbols had only been passed from mouth to ear for the purpose of teaching the Community about the Magical Universe and the Power of the androgynous, Beneficent God-dess, '*Ba'alat Gebal'*, who only ever Conceived the existence of Pure Radiant Light in Paradise. And the Wisdom of the Phoenicians reveals that what is not conceived in Heaven cannot exist in the physical world. Hence, what we now see in the material world is but the reflection of our own deluded stories which we now experience to be 'true' in our body, and by Speaking the Word to confirm our Self-Identity.

Hence, the Phoenician Philosophy of Life is easy to understand if we consider the words of '*Taautos'*, who taught that we must have 'Previous Knowledge' within us, of who we desire to be, before we will become conscious of our fulfilled desire as a physical manifestation in our world. Hence, it is impossible to be conscious of anything until it is experienced as a carnal sensation in our body, which is induced by pronouncing the sounds of the Sacred Letters.

However, devotion to the Magical androgynous God-dess began to diminish as other cultural beliefs and religious practices were introduced to the Phoenician Community and the original meaning of the Sacred Alphabet was almost forgotten. New stories now emerged which changed the intended message of the Sacred Alphabet, to reflect the ideologies of other communities living around Phoenicia, who began to use the Sacred Symbols to devise their own stories. This included the Hebrews, who adapted the Phoenician Symbols to form the Hebrew Alphabet, with which they wrote the first five books of the Hebrew Bible, known as the *'Pentateuch'*. But perhaps the original function and purpose of the Sacred Phoenician Alphabet was not fully appreciated by the Hebrews; since, according to the ancient Masters, what was originally conceived to produce only the 'Pure Consciousness of Perfection' in our world, now took on a different connotation, as we became conscious of 'good' and 'evil' in the world.

Consequently, the androgynous, self-reproducing God-dess of Pure Light was replaced by the masculine 'God of Judgement', and the simple philosophy of the Phoenicians, suddenly became more complex. For although the Hebrew 'Story of Creation' tells of the Conception of 'Pure Radiant Light' Within the Beginning, and states that 'Creation is now Finished', Genesis goes on to explain the 'creation' of Adam and Eve, and the downfall of Humanity.

73

And although the Bible today is accepted as a book which reveals the 'Creation of the World' and circumstances of the people who lived long ago, it is not actually about the physical world, or the people, but is a description of how 'Reality' is Conceived to Exist through the Power of the WORD. And while the first few verses of in Genesis are in accordance with Phoenician philosophy, which maintains that nothing but Pure Light was 'Conceived' Within the Beginning, the Hebrew version of the 'Story of Creation' in Genesis continues to tell of the 'Original Sin' which is committed by Adam and Eve in the Garden of Eden, and subsequent demise. The following passage gives a brief synopsis of the 'Seven Days of Creation,' according to the Mechanical Translation of Genesis by Benner (2007). Some words from the King James Version of the Bible (*KJV*) are included in italics for the purpose of clarification.

In the Summit (*In the Beginning KJV*) the androgynous Power's (*Elohiym*) fattened the Sky and the Land, and the Land was unfilled, and in a state of confusion and chaos. The Power/s then **Said** Light existed, and **Saw** that the Light was functional (*Good KJV*). Hence, Light and the darkness of chaos were separated, and the Light was called Day, and darkness of confusion was called night. And the evening and morning of the First Day of Creation existed, and the 'Conscious Conception of Life' is formed.

Then the androgynous Power/s **Said** a sheet will exist to separate the Water Above from the Water Below and the Power/s of *Elohiym* called the sheet, Sky (*Heaven KJV*). And evening and morning of the Second Day of Creation now existed, and the Conception of Paradise. Thus, the Power/s **Said** the water will be bound up under the Sky to one place, and dry ground will appear. The Power/s of *Elohiym* then called the dry ground, Land, and the water, Seas, and **Saw** it was functional (*Good KJV*). Then the Power/s of *Elohiym* **Said,** the Land will make all types of vegetation appear in the likeness or image of the seed of its own kind, and the Power/s **Saw** that it was functional (*Good KJV*). And the evening and morning of the Third Day of Creation now exists, and the Conception of the connection between Heaven and Earth.

The Power/s of *Elohiym* then **Said** that luminaries will exist in the Sky to make a separation between the day and the night, as signs of the appointed times, and for the days and years. Hence two magnificent luminaries appeared in the Sky to make a glow upon the land, to regulate the day, the night. And the Power/s **Saw** that it was functional (*Good KJV*). Thus, evening and morning of the Fourth Day of Creation now existed, and the Conception that the Universe is animated by Pure Vital Energy. And the Powers/s of *Elohiym* **Said** the waters will swarm with life and flyers with wings will fly upon the land and the face of the sky, and they will reproduce and increase, and fill the water and the land according to the seed of its own kind. And the Power/s **Saw** that it was functional (*Good KJV*). This was the evening and morning of the Fifth Day of Creation, and the Conception that the 'Word' is the Prophesy which causes all Life to appear. The Power/s of *Elohiym* then **Said** the land will bring forth animals according to her own kind, and **Saw** that it was functional (*Good KJV*). At which point the Power/s **Said** we will make a Human in our own Image to rule the swimmers in the seas, the flyers in the sky, and the creatures that tread upon the land. Thus, the Perfect Human, which is Pure Consciousness, was now 'Conceived' in the Image of the Power/s which is both male and female united as One. And the Power/s of *Elohiym* instructed the Perfect Human to reproduce, increase, and to fill and subdue the land and **Said** that all the trees and green herbs upon the face of the land were good for food, and the Power/s **Saw** it was functional (*Good KJV*). This is the evening and morning of the Sixth Day of Creation, when the Perfect Human was only Conscious of his Divine Inheritance from His Celestial parents.

On the Seventh Day of Creation the Conception of the sky, the land, and everything dwelling within them was finished. Thus, the Powers/s of *Elohiym* rested, and ceased Conceiving anything else. Thus, up until this moment all which is 'Conceived' is Pure Radiant Light, and the 'Vision of Perfection and Possibility' in Paradise which only existed in ethereal form; for only the potential for 'Life' was 'Conceived' by the *'Almighty Elohiym'* Within the Beginning.

However, in Chapter Two of Genesis we learn that the 'Perfect Human' which is 'Immaculately Conceived Within the Beginning', is *Yahweh* 'YHVH' (*He Exists*), who is the Pure Consciousness of the God of the Hebrews, made in the Perfect Self-Reproducing Image of *Elohiym*. And it is *'Yahweh'* who is instructed by *Elohiym* on the Sixth Day of Creation, to Subdue and Fill the Earth. Thus, *Yahweh* formed the vision of a human and blew into his nostrils the Breath of Life, and he called him *Adam* (*Moving Blood*). *Yahweh* then placed *Adam* in the Garden of Eden (*Pleasure*) where a 'Tree of Life' and a 'Tree of Discernment' or 'Judgement' (*Knowledge KJV*) were planted in the midst of the Garden, and *Yahweh* instructed *Adam* not to eat from the Tree of Discernment, for if he did, he would surely die. But *Adam* fell asleep and began dreaming that *Yahweh* had taken a rib from his body and formed *Eve* as his partner, (*meaning living*), who now appeared to *Adam* to be a separate entity from himself.

But *Eve* is actually *Adam's* own self-reflection in his 'Mirror of Truth', or his shadow made manifest in the physical world. For although *Adam* (*moving blood*)' is conceived in the Perfect Image of *Yahweh,* Who is both male and female united as One, *Adam* is now conscious of being divided, and believes himself to be separate

77

from *Eve*. Thus, the concept of duality is formed and believing it was *Eve* who was tempted by the Serpent (*deception*), and induced him to eat the Fruit from the 'Tree of Discernment', *Adam* blamed *Eve* for the 'shame' and 'guilt' he was now feeling in the blood of his body. But it was *Adam* himself who experienced the desire to eat the forbidden fruit, which resulted in him feeling 'shame' and 'guilt' because he had disobeyed *Yahweh*. And *Adam*, believing he was naked, had committed the 'Original Sin' and now became consciousness of Being something other than the Perfect Image of *Yahweh*, in Whose Pure Light he was Immaculately Conceived Within the Beginning. Thus, *Adam*, having made the choice of believing he now 'existed' somewhere other than in Paradise, became a mortal entity now living in the physical world of shadows. And *Eve*, who is the reflection of *Adam's* own perception, was now blamed for the downfall of Humanity.

Hence, *Adam* and *Eve* were now removed from the Garden in case they should eat from the 'Tree of Life' and live forever as 'gods'. Henceforth, they would have to work the ground to make a living, and all their descendants would continue to eat from the 'Tree of Discernment', and suffer the consequence of no longer living in the Garden of Eden, which resulted in pain, sickness, and death for all Humanity. But the 'Tree of Discernment' which continues to grow within us, and brings only sorrow to all who partake of its fruits is a misconception in the mind of Humanity; for only the 'Vision' of Pure Light and the Possibility of Perfection was Conceived to 'exist' by the Almighty Power/s of *Elohiym* Within the Beginning. Hence, when we choose to eat the fruit from the 'Tree of Life', which produce only Nourishing and Uplifting Sensations within us, we receive our Divine Inheritance, and now knowing we are the descendants of Pure Magical Light, we can reproduce the appearance of whatever we desire in our world. Hence, our feelings of separation, sorrow, pain, shame, guilt, and mortality, which are the forbidden fruits which grow on the 'Tree of Discernment', will disappear from our consciousness forever. For this world is only the reflection of the collective 'Vision of Humanity', which is brought to life by the Power inherent in the words that we speak while experiencing our own individual Life Story.

Both the Mechanical Translation of Genesis by Benner (2007), and the King James Version of Genesis, repeatedly use the words "**Said and Saw**", and so we can assume that since we are Conceived in the Perfect Image of the androgynous Power/s of *Elohiym*, that we too form our own world, or version of 'Reality', by '**Speaking the Word**' and '**Seeing our Vision**' as being 'Functional' and 'Good'. Therefore, we might conclude that our physical existence is the reflection of our own a story which we now consciously perceive is 'real'. But Adam is still sleeping in the Garden of Eden, and dreaming he is no longer in Paradise. And although the majority of Humanity is still asleep, some are now waking up from the dream, or nightmare, to realise that the physical world as it appears today was never conceived Within the Beginning, since the world we see all around us is only the shadow of our own Self-Conception. And as such, the physical world does not exist in the form which it appears, for what we see in the world are the solidified reflections of the stories which we have devised, and now believe are 'True'. Thus, the only way to re-claim our Divine Heritage is to re-unite with our Soul Mate in Paradise, which is the Celestial Seed of Pure Consciousness of *'Yahweh'* which Dwells within each individual, and bestows upon Humanity the Miraculous Power to reproduce our self in the Image of whatever we choose.

The Hebrew Story of Creation was later incorporated into the Christian Gospels, to tell the story of Jesus, who was Immaculately Conceived and Born of a Virgin, which was heralded by the presence of a Pure Brilliant Light in the sky. And eventually, Jesus the man is Mystically Transformed into the Elevated Consciousness of *Christ the Redeemer,* and is worshiped as an androgynous figure by early Christians, who believed that Humanity is Jesus on a Journey to our Divine Destination; the purpose of which is to become One with our Immortal Spirit, which is the *Risen Christ* within us. But until we are re-united with our 'Perfect Soul Mate in

Paradise, we deny our Divine Birth Right, by choosing to believe in delusional stories of separation and death, which now appear to be the only 'reality' in our world.

But according to the teachings of early Christianity, when we choose to ingest the physical bread and wine which signify the body and blood of Jesus, we are Mysteriously Transformed into the Perfect, Ethereal Body of the *Risen Christ*. Thus, the sensations of Peace and True Love that are induced within us, which are the Fruits that grow on the 'Tree of Life', Miraculously Convert our physical body from within, into the Image of our own Messiah, now living in Paradise. Thus, when we are One with our Inner Soul Mate, we become the 'Holy Grail', which is the Vessel containing the 'Blood of our Saviour'. And the Passion aroused within us by re-enacting this drama awakens parts of our DNA which presently lie dormant, and changes our Conscious perception of our Self and the world. However, the dogmatic teachings of the Christian Church today bear no resemblance to the original Phoenician Ideologies of Peace, True Love and Forgiveness, which are the basic Principles that early Christianity were originally founded upon.

Nevertheless, the adapted form of the Letters of the original Sacred Alphabet, which we still use today to form Words to tell our own Life Story, reveal the Magical Powers concealed within the sound of every Word we speak. And when our Life Story is in accordance with the beneficent qualities of the Divine Light within us, we will have no need for outer mentors. gurus, priests, or religious dogmas to teach us the 'True Meaning of Life'; for our instruction will come directly from within our own Heart.

There are many stories and systems now in the world to 'assist' in the development of our 'self-awareness', however some of these self-help theories are so complicated that we have become bogged down by the dogma which surrounds them, and have now lost sight of the original simple message which is revealed by the Sacred Phoenician Alphabet. Hence, the original meaning of the Sacred Symbols and Letters has almost been lost or disregarded as new philosophies and scientific theories have been devised to explain the 'Miracle of Creation'. But the Principle of Pure Light, which represents 'Self-Knowledge will always depend on our own conscious perception. And it is the sensation that we feel within us which decides our 'Reality'; for we either feel that we are now the person who we desire to be, or we do not, since there is no other state in between. Hence, it is the sensations impressed as memories on our DNA which determines our 'State of Consciousness' and continued existence; since our mind can only recall the memory of sensations which have already been experienced within our body.

Incidentally, it was also prophesied by ancient storytellers that eventually Humanity will become conscious of an 'Elevated State of 'Bliss', when in the Silence within our own Heart we will become conscious of 'existing', but not as any particular 'thing' or 'person'. And this State of Elevated Consciousness is represented by the Phoenician Symbol of **SIMS**, which was never spoken out loud in order to preserve and protect the Purity and Perfection of the Mother God-dess. Therefore, **SIMS** is not included in the Twenty-Two Letters of the 'Process of Creation'. However, the Magical Symbol of **SIMS** was known by the Phoenicians as the 'Star Seed of Pure Light' inherited from our Celestial Ancestors who founded a civilization on Planet Earth of people with Extraordinary Magical Skills. And it is this un-seen Star Seed of Pure Light at the Heart of every individual, which bestows upon Humanity the 'Knowledge' to continually reproduce our self in our own Image.

Hence, the Jews never make any physical representations of the Divine, or pronounce the Name of God in full, and always write the word 'God' as 'G-d' in scripts, which is in keeping with ancient tradition. Nevertheless, there is a great difference between the Phoenician and Hebrew interpretation of the attributes of 'G-d'; since the Hebrews suggested that both 'light' and 'darkness', and 'good' and 'evil' can exist within 'G-d'. While the Phoenicians maintained there is only one Power in the Magical Universe, and that is the Unseen, Undivided, Pure Consciousness of the Benign, Self-Reproducing God-dess of Radiant Light, which is all that is 'Conceived to Exist' Within the Beginning. And everything which appears to be otherwise is in the un-focused 'Eye of the Beholder'.

Thankfully, after telling the story of how Humanity came to be entangled in the physical world of shadows, the Hebrews also devised stories to teach us the Way to regain the Pure Conscious State of Enlightenment in Paradise, in the form of the 'Mystical Kabbalah' and the 'Art of Astrology'. But as we shall see, these stories have also been dramatically changed by subsequent generations who have added their own, and often misguided interpretations, of the original intention of these stories.

The Sacred Alphabet and the Kabbalah

The 'Mystical Kabbalah', sometimes 'spelled' as 'Qabalah', is the 'Way of Wisdom' which gives instruction on how we might transform our self, and the world in which we live, by balancing the forces of nature through gaining knowledge of the Symbols and Letters of the Sacred Alphabet and the 'Tree of Life', also known as the 'Otz Chim'. The story of Kabbalah is based on the Phoenician Symbol of **SIN** 手, which is the original 'Tree of Life' that gives Humanity the opportunity to change our present stories of sorrow and tragedy, and to witness the amazing possibilities which become apparent when we choose to eat the wholesome fruit from the 'Tree of Life', which induces only nourishing vibrations and miraculous sensations in our Heart and Body.

But the Phoenician 'Tree of Life', which was depicted by the simple symbol of **SIN** 手, only had three branches that were considered to be the Three Divine Attributes of the Mother God-dess. These were represented by the Almighty Letter **AL** which is Pure Light of 'Nothingness', that is suspended on the central branch of the 'Tree', and decides between **MAH** (*Manifestation*), on the lower branch of the 'Tree', and **SHIN** (*Dissolution*), hung on the upper branch, with which any story or prophecy can be devised, or altered, to reveal our own particular desired ending to our Life Story.

Original Phoenician Symbol of SIN as the 'Tree of Life'

Upper Branch - SHIN - *Fire*

Centre Branch - AL - *Air*

Lower Branch - MAH - *Water*   *Fig 1.*

However, Kabbalists later chose to make the 'Tree of Life', and the 'Process of Creation' more complex, either out of ignorance or by design, possibly to keep the Ancient Wisdom from the masses. Hence, a 'Tree of Life' was devised on which Twenty-Two Paths were suspended on Ten Ethereal Sephirot of 'Nothingness', which are Emanations of Light, through which the Pure Radiant Light of Heaven descends to Earth at the speed of Lightning. The Twenty-Two Paths consist of the three original horizontal Paths, which represent the Mother Letters, (*AL, MEM,* and *SHIN*); seven upright Paths that are synonymous with the Seven States of Consciousness, that are alleged by Kabbalists to manifest as either 'good' or 'evil' in our world; and also twelve diagonal Paths, which are the Virtues that must be assimilated within us in order to change our conscious perception of 'reality'. But more recently the Ten Ethereal Sephirot were also included as Paths, making Thirty-Two Paths in all.

The Flash of Lightening emanates from the *'Ayin Soph Aur'*, which is the Limitless Radiant Light that is within, and all around us in our Magical Universe. Nevertheless, the Limitless Light of *'Ain Soph Aur'* cannot be attained by Humanity while we are still only conscious of existing as a sperate entity in the physical world of shadows. For the Light of *'Ain Soph Aur'*, refers to the Magical Light of our Divine Ancestors who came from the Stars to found a miraculous civilisation on Earth that would work together as 'One Divine Being' to reveal the Pure Light of Paradise in our world.

The *'Sefer Yetzirah'* or *'Book of Creation'*, (Kaplan 1997), is allegedly one of the first ancient scripts to have been recorded concerning the teaching of Kabbalah and Astrology, which is thought to have been written by the Patriarch Abraham, around 1800B.C. However, there is some speculation that the original *'Sefer Yetzirah'* may not have ever been a written document, but was a story passed from mouth to ear, according to the tradition of that day. And that Abraham's version of the *'Sefer Yetzirah'* may have only consisted of 240 words at its original conception. Nevertheless, there are now several versions of the *'Sefer Yetzirah'* and many of these translations contain up to 2500 words; thus incorporating teachings which could not have possibly been included in the original story which comprised of only 240 words. The *'Sefer Yetzirah'* explains the meaning of the Book of Genesis in the Bible, by equating the 'Seven

Days of Creation' with the teachings of the Mystical Kabbalah and the Art of Astrology to describe the Magical Process of Creation through the Twenty-Two Symbols and Letters of the Sacred Alphabet. But the original purpose of both the Mystical Kabbalah and Astrology are no longer appreciated by the majority of Humanity, since many features have now been added to the original stories that were not practiced by ancient people.

These additions are too numerous to mention, but include 'naming' the Ten Sephirot in Kabbalah, which were originally understood to be 'Emanations of Pure Light, in which 'Nothing' existed, not even the sound of a name; for naming something suggests that it has physical substance and is observable. And an eleventh Sephirah, known as 'Daath', was incorporated into the original diagram of the 'Tree of Life' by later generations of Kabbalists. (See Fig, 9) Also our understanding of Astrology has been influenced with the discovery of the outer planets, Neptune, Uranus and Pluto, which were not known to ancient people. Added to this there are the ever-changing interpretations given to ancient texts as 'new information' comes to light, which is often the opinion of a translator who may have little knowledge or understanding of the original intention of the Sacred Phoenician Alphabet, Kabbalah, and Astrology, but nevertheless these stories are now accepted as being 'true' by many scholars of the Mystical Arts.

There are several ancient legends based on the 'Tree of Life' which suggest that the original 'Tree of Life' is a representation of the 'Primordial Light of Creation' that was regarded as the Infinite Wisdom of a Feminine Deity which pre-dates the 'Story of Creation' in the Bible. Later interpretations of this legend name the Feminine Divinity as the '**Shekinah**', derived from the Hebrew root word '**Shekha**', meaning 'to Dwell', and it is the ethereal '*Shekinah*' which gives birth to the Divine Spark of Light within each individual. However, the '*Shekinah*' is also associated with the 'Serpent of Deception', which is said to have tempted *Eve* to eat the forbidden fruit in the Garden of Eden, that marked the descent of Humanity from Heaven into the physical world of shadows. Nevertheless, contrary to popular belief, Kabbalah was not originally based on any particular earthly religion, but is an ancient perspective of our Magical Heritage bequeathed to us from our Celestial Ancestors. And there is some speculation which suggests that the modern version of Kabbalah may only have been devised during the first century A.D.

The philosophy of Kabbalah, like all Spiritual Traditions, teaches us that the Light in the Kingdom of Heaven is already present on Earth, if only we have the eyes to see; since the world around us is Pure Vital Energy vibrating at various velocities, which appears to our eyes as physical manifestations, according to our perception and present state of consciousness. The study of Kabbalah is usually divided into three categories; *Theoretical Kabbalah*, which is mostly concerned with the Hierarchy of Angelic Beings in the Upper World; *Meditative Kabbalah*, which uses the resonant sounds produced when speaking the Sacred Letters to form the 'Names of 'G-d' to induce Divine Sensations in our Heart and body; and *Practical Kabbalah* which is said to influence events apparently happening in the world through the Power of Magic. Kabbalah also assigns a numerical value to each Letter, and Words which add up to the equivalent numerical value are thought to reveal the same Divine Attribute of G-d.

The Numerical Value of the Letters

1.	ꤰ	AL =	1 (1000)	12.	Ɬ	LAM =	30
2.	ꔷ	BET =	2	13.	ᴀᴀᴀ	MAH =	40
3.	Ꝇ	GAM =	3	14.	ꓔ	NUN =	50
4.	ꓔ	DA L =	4	15.	ꤲ	SIN =	60
5.	ꢁ	HEY =	5	16.	◉	AYIN =	70
6.	Ƴ	VAV =	6	17.	◯	PEY =	80
7.	ꓕ	ZAN =	7	18.	ꝋꓵ	TSAD =	90
8.	ꛉ	HHETS = 8		19.	⊖	QUPH =	100
9.	⊗	THET =	9	20.	ꡘ	RESH =	200
10.	ꔾ	YAD =	10	21.	Ꮤ	SHIN =	300
11.	Ɯ	KAPH = 20		22.	✝	TAW =	400

The teaching of the Mystical Kabbalah in the *'Sefer Yetzirah'* is founded upon the Seven Days of Creation, which is an account of the Seven States of Consciousness that must be developed in order to produce a Perfect Human Being on Earth. And the Kabbalah is a system of instruction on how to balance the forces of nature to cause the 'Lightening Flash' in Heaven to descend to Earth in order to 'create' a 'Golem'; which according to the Hebrews is a physical being made of clay, brought to life through the Power of Magic for the purpose of 'Doing the Will of the Creator' in the world. Thus, by Ascending the Tree and assimilating the Perfect Virtues of the Sacred Alphabet we become 'Enlightened', and realise that it is we who are the Golem, and that our purpose in life is to carry out the 'Will of the Creator' by reproducing our own Paradise on Earth.

But while we still have feelings of anger, guilt, revenge, regret, shame, poverty, ill-health etc., which are signs that we are not yet resonating with our Ideal State in Heaven, we cannot possibly reveal the Pure Light of Paradise in our world, until we acknowledge that we are solely responsible for our own pain and sorrow. This concept is based on the original Phoenician pictograph of **SIN** 丰 that represents our Protection and Defence against the 'Sharp Seeds' which are growing in our Garden within us, and are the cause of our present suffering. But the Letter **SIN** has now become associated with 'wrongdoing' and 'sinfulness', instead of being our protection from pain and sorrow, as it was originally conceived to be by the Phoenicians. Thus, the story of 'Original Sin' emerged with the first human *Adam* in the Garden of Eden, who eating the fruit from the 'Tree of Discernment' after being instructed by *Yahweh* to only eat from the 'Tree of Life', felt 'shame' and 'guilt' for being naked. And *Adam*, wanting to appear innocent before 'God', went on to compound the situation by blaming his ill-considered actions on *Eve*; who is really only a reflection of *Adam* in the world. Hence, the term 'Original Sin' lives on as a memory in the DNA of Humanity, and will continue to be so until we alter our understanding of '**Sin**', and change our perception of 'reality '.

Mistakenly, when the Hebrews adapted the Symbols of the Sacred Phoenician Alphabet to formulate the Letters of the Hebrew Alphabet, although they inherited some of the Beneficent Stories and Legends of the ancient Phoenicians, they also added their own theories to the original meaning of the letters, to reflect their beliefs and ideologies. Hence, the true function and purpose of the Sacred Symbols and Letters was no longer fully understood, since many erroneous stories and notions of 'darkness' and 'evil' were now introduced to the original benign conception of the Phoenicians Letters; which were based on the knowledge that only the Presence of Pure Life Sustaining Light exists in our Magical Universe.

However, since the 'Tree of Life' is a representation of our Magical Inheritance of Self-Reproduction Inherited from our Celestial Ancestors, the Hebrews, like all Humanity, were free to devise any story which they desired to become a 'reality'. For by Suspending our story on the Ten Ineffable Sephirot of Pure Magical Light, all stories will miraculously appear in physical form in our world. And the appearance or disappearance of any story depends on the three Mother Letters; **AL** *(Air)*, **MAH** *(Water)*, and **SHIN** *(Fire)*. For it is the Letter **'AL'**, which is the Ethereal Element of Air that represents the Breath in our Word, which decides between 'Manifestation' through the Letter **MAH**, that is synonymous with the Ethereal Element of Water, or the 'Dissolution' of an appearance by the Ethereal Element of Fire, which is represented by the Letter **'SHIN'**.

And as we go through the 'Process of Self-Creation', we assimilate the vibrations in our body of the Twelve Virtues of the Zodiac which are synonymous with the Sacred Letters; **HEY** *(Aries)*, **VAV** *(Taurus)*, **ZAN** *(Gemini)*, **HHETS** *(Cancer)*, **THET** *(Leo)*, **YAD** *(Virgo)*, **LAM** *(Libra)*, **NUN** *(Scorpio)*, **SIN** *(Sagittarius)*, **AYIN** *(Capricorn)*, **TSAD** *(Aquarius)*, and **QUPH** *(Pisces)*. Hence, the Seven Stages of Conscious Development, signified by the Sacred Letters and Planets; **BET** *(Saturn)*, **GAM** *(Jupiter)*, **DAL** *(Mars)*, **KAPH** *(Sun)*, **PEY** *(Venus)*, **RESH** *(Mercury)* and **TAW** *(Moon)*, are a natural consequence of our Celestial, Self-Reproductive Power within us.

However, the original 'Tree of Life' of the Phoenicians, which only produces Nourishing Fruit that grows in abundance and is freely available for all who choose to eat it, was no longer the only Tree in the Garden of Eden; since the 'Tree of Discernment' was introduced in the Hebrew 'Story of Creation', along with the concept of 'Good' and 'Evil'. For while the 'Tree of Life' gives Sustenance, Healing, and Immortality to all who choose to eat of its Fruits, partaking of the fruits from the 'Tree of Discernment' only offers the possibility of duality, pain, sorrow, and eventual death. But according to Phoenician philosophy, only Pure Radiant Light was 'Conceived to Exist' Within the Beginning. Therefore, the potential for seeing the 'Perfection in Everything' is already inherent within Humanity, if we choose to perceive it that way. And since there is only One Power in the Universe, all that is needed to manifest our fulfilled desire in the world is to eat the Nourishing Fruit from the 'Tree of Life', which means to only feel the presence of 'Good Vibrations' in our Heart and Body, and remain perfectly still as we witness the Miraculous appearance of our own Paradise on Earth.

The following diagrams illustrate how the 'Tree of Life' has become a more complex with each subsequent translation of the original 'Sefer Yetzirah'; hence, the 'Tree of Life' no longer represents the simple Phoenician Symbol of the Sacred Letter '**SIN**'.

Original 'Tree of Life'

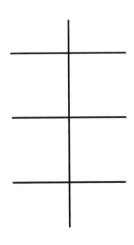

Fig.2

Twenty-Two Paths

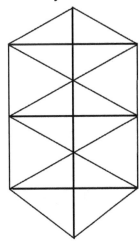

Fig. 3

22 Paths plus 10 Sephirot

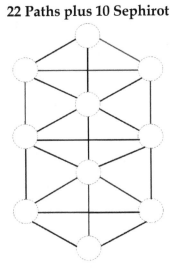

Fig. 4

Lightening Flash

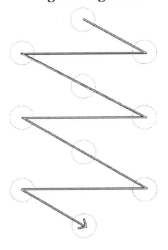

Fig.5

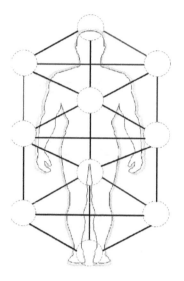

A human figure superimposed on the 'Tree of Life' which consists of Ten Ethereal Sephirot and 22 Paths, making 32 Paths. The 3 cross lines represent the 3 Mother Letters, the 7 upright lines signify the 7 Fathers, or States of Consciousness, and the 12 diagonal lines are the Virtues which we must experience within us to bring the Magic of Heaven to Earth.

Fig. 6

Once the Ten Sephirot were included as paths, the 'Tree' now has Thirty -Two paths in all. But the concept that the Sephirot are actual physical paths is misleading, since a Sephirah was originally an Ethereal Emanation of Light which has no observable substance, and therefore cannot be justifiably described as a 'Path' in the physical sense. For only the Twenty-Two Letters produce specific vibrations which result in physical manifestations. Thus, the Ten Ineffable Emanations of Pure Light of the Sephirot, which have 'Limitless Depth' but no physical mass, do not equate with any Letter, Symbol, Number, or indeed anything that can be described in Words; even though many Kabbalists have attempted to do so since the story of Kabbalah was first conceived by Abraham.

In this respect all early versions of the *'Sefer Yetzirah'* are in agreement, since they all state clearly that there are only 'Ten Ineffable Sephirot', and not nine or eleven, which are 'Emanations of Pure Light', with no physical substance, and are therefore described as being 'Nothing', *(from the Hebrew word 'Belimar', meaning 'Nothingness')*. However, later Kabbalists continue to bestow upon the Sephirot many connotations and names to distinguish them from each other, which implies that the Ethereal Sephirot possess physical characteristics.

And any name which implies a specific limited, physical, condition, will impress upon us preconceived notions about the nature of that 'thing'. But it is only through the illusive nature of the Ten Ineffable Sephirot that we experience the 'Higher Realms of Consciousness', and receive 'Knowledge and 'Guidance', which according to tradition is only revealed through the Ethereal Sensations that we feel in our Heart. Thus, ultimately the Essence of the Ten Ineffable Sephirot is indefinable in words, since their true nature can only be experienced within each individual. And if we begin our study of Kabbalah with an inaccurate understanding of the meaning of the Ten Illusive Sephirot, then these concepts are bound to influence our learning, and may even impede the progress of our 'Journey to our Divine Destination'. But once we have assimilated the Twelve Virtues of the Zodiac, and have attained the Seven States of

Consciousness represented by the Planets, the 'Lightning Flash' will descend from Heaven through the Ten Illusive Sephirot and Illuminated our World.

In modern Kabbalah the Ten Ineffable Sephirot are usually represented by the names shown on the list on the following page, which are often considered to be presided over by the Archangels, who are in themselves Ethereal, but suggest various services that they perform for 'God' which can vary considerably, according to the person who is telling the story.

Names of the Ten Sephirot and Archangels

1. **Kether**   **Metatron:** Angel of the Divine Presence
2. **Chokma**   **Ratziel:** The Herald of God
3. **Binah**   **Tzaphkiel:** The Watcher of God
4. **Chesed**   **Tzadkiel:** The Righteous of God
5. **Geburah**   **Khamael:** The Burner of God
6. **Tipareth**   **Raphael:** The Healer of God
7. **Netzach**   **Auriel:** I, The God
8. **Hod**   **Michael:** The Defender of God
9. **Yesod**   **Gabriel:** The Strong one of God
10. **Malkut**   **Sandalphon:** The Sound of Sandals

There are also Four Worlds on the modern version of the 'Tree of Life' namely; '*Atziluth*, World of Emanation' *(Nothingness)*; '*Briah*, World of Creation', *(Something from Nothing)*; '*Yetzirah*, World of Formation', *(Something from Something)*; '*Asiyah*, World of Manifestation', *(Completion)*, which all appear to be separated like layers of an onion, with each successive layer vibrating at a slower rate of frequency, therefore appearing to be more material in nature than the previous layer. But all the apparent sperate layers are merged together as One Whole Entity, implying that the 'World of Emanation' is always present in the 'World of Manifestation'. Therefore, wherever we may believe we are in the Universe, the Pure Magical Light of our Celestial Ancestors is always within, and all around us, which can cause the appearance of any possibility to miraculously manifest on Earth at the speed of Lightening, when we are Conscious of our own Divine Heritage.

The Four Worlds of Creation According to Kabbalah

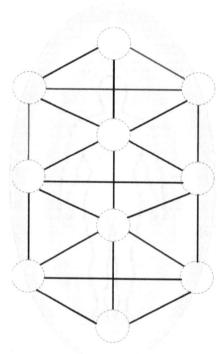

ATZILUT – 'World of Emanation' (Illumination/'Nothingness

BRIAH – 'World of Creation (Conception/Something from 'Nothing')

YETZIRAH – 'World of Formation' (Sensation/ Something from Something)

ASIYAH – 'World of Physical Manifestation' (Expression/Action/ Completion)

Fig. 7

In *Fig. 8* we see that each Path on the 'Tree of Life' is assigned a Letter, with which most Kabbalists are not in agreement, but are arranged here according to Rabbi Gaon, c. 1800AD. However, since the Sacred Letters were originally devised so that we might form Words to tell our own unique Life Story, the Sacred Letters should be arranged on the 'Tree' to reveal our personal Journey to our Divine Destination, and not be according to another person's story.

Ten Sephirot, Twenty-Two Letters & Paths on the Tree of Life

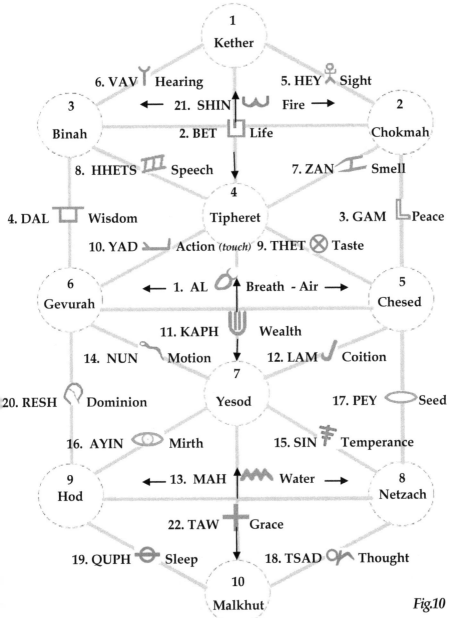

Fig.10

According to Rabbi Eliahu Gaon of Vilna, c.1800AD. (Gra Version)

The modern 'Tree of Life' is now depicted as also having Three Pillars, known as the 'Pillar of Mercy', the 'Pillar of Severity', and the 'Pillar of Equilibrium'. The 'Pillar of Mercy' begins at *Chokmah* and descends through *Chesed* to *Netzach*, and is to our right when observing the diagram face on, but to our left if we are observing our world with our back to the 'Tree'. The 'Pillar of Severity' begins at *Binah* and descends through *Gevurah* to *Hod*, and is to our left if we are observing the diagram, but to our right when observing the world from the 'Tree'. And the 'Pillar of Equilibrium' begins at *Kether* and descends through *Daath, Tipharet, Yesod*, to *Malkut*, and is at the Centre of the Tree. Thus, we are told that the 'Process of Self-Creation' is much faster and easier when we Ascend the 'Tree' by the 'Middle Pillar of Equilibrium'. However, the Three Pillars are not mentioned in early translations of the '*Sefer Yetzirah*', and are only seen in later versions of Kabbalah.

The 'Tree of Life' has been embellish even further by adding 231 Gates which we must enter by combining the Twenty-Two Sacred Letters together in sequence to manifest our desires, or dissolve any outworn physical conditions that are no longer required. Thus, it is obvious that these details that were not included in the original version of the '*Sefer Yetzirah*', which may have contained as few as 240 words, and did not mention of the Three Pillars and the 231 Gates, which can only be the invention of later Kabbalists.

However, no matter how complex and mysterious the Teachings of the 'Mystical Kabbalah' and the 'Tree of Life' have become, it has served to keep the original message of the Phoenicians alive in the Hearts and Minds of the people. For Kabbalah conveys the message that our world is transient in nature and that anything is possible in the physical world of shadows; for our 'reality' is founded on our own personal stories which we tell and have come to believe are 'true', Hence, from an oral teaching tradition that was handed down to the community by word of mouth from spiritual scholars, the Story of Kabbalah has since been elaborated upon by each subsequent generation, until today the *'Sefer Yetzirah'* has now grown in volume from the original 240 words to well over two thousand words in more recent translations.

And it was possibly the Kabbalists of the 18th Century A.D. who introduced many of these changes to the original teachings of 'Kabbalah', including the eleventh Sephirah on the 'Tree of Life', known as *Daath*, which they suggested is not really a Sephirot, but the point of convergence between 'Wisdom' and 'Understanding', as seen in *Fig. 9.* Nevertheless, according to Kabbalah, before our 'Tree' will bear fruit in our world we must first assimilate within us Twelve Virtues and Seven States of Consciousness, by inducing the Sensations of the Sacred Alphabet. Thus once all the Twenty-Two Paths on the 'Tree of Life' are connected through the Ten Ethereal

Sephirot, our 'Tree' will be illuminated like a 'Christmas Tree' as we Receive the Gifts of Heaven; for we are now a clear channel for the 'Lightening Flash' to descend to Earth and reveal the story that we desire to become manifest in our world. Hence, a Magical Transformation takes place within us as our world is miraculously changed to reflect the Perfect Image of our Fulfilled Heart's desire, and the realisation of our own Heaven on Earth.

But how much more simplified is the Phoenician 'Tree of Life', where 'SIN' is only a misconception, and all that we need to do to change our perception of 'reality' is to alter our own story by Ascending the 'Tree' to See our world from a different perspective, while feeling the sensation of already living in our Paradise on Earth. However, the diagram on t, Fig.9, shows the more complex modern version of the 'Tree of Life', devised by later Kabbalists, which illustrates the 'Fall of Humanity' and the pseudo Sephirot of Daath. Also, the Ten original Sephirot are now included as 'Paths' 1 to 10, while the Twenty-Two Paths shown on Fig. 8, are now numbered 11 to 32, making 'Thirty-Two Paths'.

Modern Version of the Tree of Life Including Daath

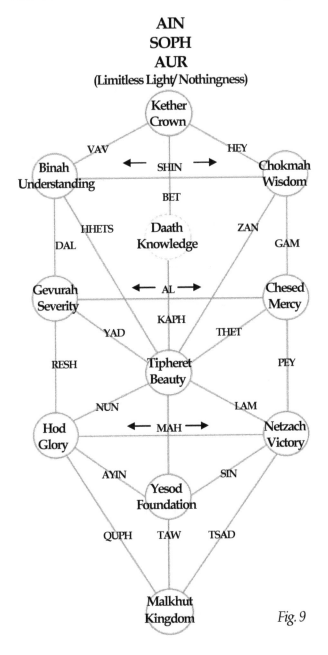

AIN
SOPH
AUR
(Limitless Light/Nothingness)

Kether
Crown

VAV   HEY
Binah   ← SHIN →   Chokmah
Understanding   Wisdom
BET

HHETS   Daath   ZAN
DAL   Knowledge   GAM

Gevurah   ← AL →   Chesed
Severity   Mercy
KAPH
YAD   THET

RESH   Tipheret   PEY
Beauty

NUN   LAM
Hod   ← MAH →   Netzach
Glory   Victory

AYIN   SIN
Yesod
Foundation

QUPH   TAW   TSAD

Malkhut   *Fig. 9*
Kingdom

Thus, the Wisdom of the Mystical Kabbalah reveals that we must each form our own 'Tree of Life' within us, by devising words with the Twenty-Two Letters of the Sacred Alphabet to tell the story of our own Miraculous Journey to our Divine Destination. For the 'Magical Tree of Life' constantly grows within each Human Being, and bears fruit according to the Seed which is implanted in our DNA, through the sensations we feel in our Heart and Body. And since the material world is suspended on the Ten Ineffable Sephirot which are 'Emanations of Pure Light', or 'Nothingness', our physical world may not be as solid as it appears. However, the ever-changing story of Kabbalah has served to keep alive the Wisdom of the Ancient Masters; which is that we each form our own version of 'reality' through the resonance of the Words which we Speak and what we now Perceive to be 'Real'.

The original 'Tree of Life' has been dramatically altered since the simple conception of the Phoenician Symbol of SIN ⌗, with only three branches which represent the Three aspects of the Mother God-dess, to a more complex version with Thirty-Two Paths, plus an Eleven Sephirot of **Daath**. But the original Phoenician form of the 'Tree of Life' was adapted by the Hebrews to represent the 'Fall of Humanity' from the 'State of Grace in Heaven', into the physical world of shadows below, because of the 'Original Sin' perceived to have been committed by *Adam*. Henceforth, all subsequent generations are said to still be suffering the repercussions of the actions of *Adam*. And it is this version of the 'Tree of Life' which now has many advocates, but also several critics who maintain that the original pattern of the Tree should not be altered. For although the Fruit on the 'Tree of Life' continues to grow, and changes form and appearance, according to our desires and personal choices, the original method of producing the vibration of the Virtues will remain unchanged throughout Eternity. And the 'Original Tree of Life' of the Phoenicians already contains the pattern for every 'Seed' or 'Story' that we could possibly desire to manifest as a 'reality' in our Paradise on Earth. And all we have to do to change our world is to bear witness to the manifestation of the Desired Ending of our story, which is activated through the Sensations we feel in our Heart and Body, and confirmed by our own Spoken Word; while not reacting to what now appears 'real' in our world.

The original *'Sefer Yetzirah'* may have contained as few as 240 words, and the following poem gives an example in 240 words, of the story possibly told by the Patriarch Abraham around 1800B.C.

The Tree of Life in 240 Words

Ten Ineffable Sephirot of 'Nothingness';

Three Mother Letters of AL, MAH, and SHIN;

Seven Fathers, Conceived by the Mothers;

and Twelve Virtues which save us from 'Sin',

all suspended on the 'Magical Tree of Life'

which grows forever in our World Within.

Naught is said of the Mystical Sephirot,

except they are 'Ten' Emanations of Light

through which all is Engraved and Carved,

and in a Flash of Lightening, is revealed to our Sight.

For each Endless Sephirah conceals the 'Truth'

of our Celestial Heritage and Magical Birth-right.

The Three Mother Letters at the Heart of the 'Tree'

are **AL**, which is the *Breath* that decides on Creation,

while **MAH**, is the *Water* of Manifestation,

and **SHIN**, is the *Fire* of Dissolution and our Liberation.

Thus, all in existence is revealed by the 'Word',

spoken with Passion and Benevolent Intention.

The Seven Stages of Consciousness are **BET**, *Life*;
GAM, *Peace*; **DAL**, *Wisdom*; **KAPH**, *Wealth*;
PEY, *Seed*, **RESH**, *Dominion*; and **TAW**, *Amazing Grace*,
through which we receive Prosperity and Good Health.
And when all Stages of Consciousness are Unified as One,
our body of clay is Transformed with Stealth.

The Twelve Virtues needed to complete this task
are **HEY**, *Sight*; **VAV**, *Hearing*; **ZAN**, *Smell*;
HHETS, *Speech*; **THET**, *Taste*; **YAD**, *Action*; and **LAM**,
the *Coition* of Heaven and Earth, in which we dwell;
NUN, *Motion*; **SIN**, *Moderation*; **AYIN**, *Mirth*; **TSAD**, *Thought*;
while **QUPH** is to *Sleep* in Paradise, Knowing All Is Well.

This account of the 'Wisdom of Kabbalah' is an introduction to the 'Western Mystery Tradition' and the 'Magical Arts', and there are now many books in circulation, and also much information on the Internet for interested readers. However, they don't tell the same simple story as the original version of the '*Sefer Yetzirah*', known as the '*Book of Creation*', in 240 words, and therefore any serious student of Kabbalah must find their own 'Truth' within their Heart.

True Art of Astrology

The Patriarch Abraham, who is attributed as being the original story teller of Kabbalah, is also known as the 'Father of Astrology', since it is believed it was Abraham who first saw the correlation between the Letters of the Sacred Alphabet, the Planets, and the Zodiac. Thus, suggesting that everything in existence is impressed with the same pattern of vibration which is evident in the Heavens at the moment when someone takes their first breath in the physical world. However, the practice of Astrology, in one form or another, possibly predates Abraham by thousands of years; since mankind has probably always gazed at the night sky and devised amazing stories about the life of the Planets and Stars, which they related to the attributes of the Divine Celestial Ancestors of Humanity. And the stories tell of the drama constantly being performed in Heaven as the Planets move through the 'Circle of Life', known as the 'Zodiac' which means 'Band of Animals'. However, it is not the physical appearance of the animals that was being considered, but their potential strengths and innate Magical Powers. Hence, each of the Twelve Signs of the Zodiac corresponds with a Perfect Virtue which must be developed and assimilated within us before the Pure Consciousness of the Seven known Planets can express their Magic through us. For only the Sun, Moon, Mercury, Venus, Mars, Jupiter, and Saturn were recognised by ancient Astrologers, since Uranus, Neptune and Pluto were only discovered more recently.

The Zodiac is a representation of the Pure Light in Heaven refracted through a prism, which appears on Earth as twelve colours, or shades, with different vibrations and qualities. And mistakenly, most people today believe that the practice of Astrology is founded on the placement of the Planets in the Constellations, which is a misunderstanding; since the 'Zodiac' no longer corresponds to the backdrop of the Constellations, as it once did when the 'Story of Astrology was first conceived by Abraham, due to the 'Precession of the Equinoxes.

Precession of the Equinoxes *A westward shift of the equinoxes along the plane of the ecliptic at a rate of 50.27 seconds of arc a year, resulting from precession of the earth's axis of rotation, and causing the equinoxes to occur earlier each sidereal year. Thus, the Zodiac is no longer in alignment with the original Constellation that it was when the story of the Zodiac was first devised and observed.*

Thus, the Twelve Signs of the Zodiac are Ethereal in nature, having no physical substance, but represent the godlike Virtues of the 'Star People' who are our Celestial Ancestors that came to Earth long before Abraham was born. And the Planets represent the 'Wisdom' and 'Knowledge of Magic', that is the State of Pure Consciousness of our Ancestors, which Humanity will Inherit once we have assimilated each of the Perfect Virtues of the Zodiac.

According to an ancient Mesopotamian legend, the most important Celestial Body in the Heavens is the Sun (*Son*), that was known as *Anki*, the first born of the androgynous God-dess *Namma*, who is on His journey through the Zodiac to his Divine Destination (*destiny*), to take up his rightful place as Ruler of the Kingdom of Heaven and Earth. And the first Sign of the Zodiac, which is Aries, begins when the Sun (*Son*) crosses over from Pisces to Aries in springtime, known as the Vernal Equinox, which is the time to plant seeds when the Earth is fertile. And springtime is still celebrated today as Easter by Christians, at the first Full Moon following the Vernal Equinox, unusually in March or early April. The Jews also hold a celebration around this time of year, known as the 'Passover' that originally marked the change in the seasons, with the end of Winter and beginning of Spring when day and night are of equal length. And eventually the 'Celebration of the Passover' became linked to the Exodus of the Israelites crossing over the Red Sea.

The 21st day of June is the Summer Solstice, when the Sun is in Cancer in the Northern Hemisphere, and at its nearest point to the Earth, which by now is in full bloom and the days are long, warmed by the vibrant life-giving rays of the Sun (*Son*). By September the Sun is in Libra when day and night are once again of equal length at the Autumnal Equinox, which is celebrated by giving thanks and gratitude to the Mother and the Sun (*Son*) for the harvest which has already been gathered, and stored in readiness for Winter.

As the Sun begins to retreat from the Earth the days become shorter and the Sun is furthest away from the Earth when everything appears to be dormant. But during these dark days the Sun (*Son*) is being nourished and replenished by the Magical Essence of his Mother, until on December 21st at the Winter Solstice in Capricorn, the Sun begins to return to the Earth and the days start to lengthen. Hence, the greatest celebration of the year now takes place; for the Son has returned from His sabbatical with the Divine Mother and brings with Him the Miraculous Light which shines brightly in the Heavens, announcing the Advent of the *Son*, who is the Light in our World who is born to be King. At this season of the year Christmas is celebrated by Christians, which was known as Saturnalia by some other religious sects. And from December until March/April the Earth is increasingly bathed in Magical Light, as everything is prepared in readiness for when the Sun crosses over from Pisces to

Aries, and the old Cycle of the Year comes to an end, as a new year begins.

Hence, it became a tradition among ancient people that the placement of the Planets in the Heavens was considered at the moment a Son was born who was destined to become Leader or King, to assess his 'Godlike Virtues', and 'Divine Right to Rule'. The smaller Cycle of the Sun, which marks the day and night, represents the Sun and the King Ruling the Earth during the day, and the merging of the King's Soul with the Sun at night to be replenished by the Mother, until together they arise renewed in the morning. Thus, the Stars and Planets in the 'Story of Creation' in Genesis are Immaculately Conceived in Heaven on the Fourth Day of Creation, when it was Declared that the Sun and Moon would Shine Light to regulate the Seasons of the Year and the Days of the Week. And everything was seen to be 'functioning perfectly'; for whatever is conceived to be 'true' in the Inner World will always be reflected in the outer world of shadows.

Most modern Astrologers still use the concept of the Journey of the Sun and Planets through the Zodiac, in order to inform clients of their probable Identity (*psychological characteristics*), and possible destination (*Destiny*). However, to ancient Astrologers, the Planets and the Signs of the Zodiac were not originally conceived to convey any adverse qualities, since everything is 'Created Perfect' Within the Beginning, Thus following the 'Old Ways of the Ancestors, the ancient Astrologers believed that nothing 'bad' could possibly happen to the King while on his Journey to his Divine Destination, and if anything undesirable did appear to transpire, it could be changed by 'Speaking the Word' to alter their perception of 'reality'. And with the same abiding Faith that the Sun would rise every morning, they knew that everything needed for a prosperous and healthy life style would always be provided by the God-dess through Her Perfect Son; which is the Immortal Spirit, or Star Seed of Pure Light which dwells at the Heart of every human being. Therefore, if the energies of the Planets and Signs of the Zodiac appear flawed, or to portend malefic events, it is because of our lack of knowledge, and misguided perception.

As the stories concerning the true nature of 'reality' became more complex, the Planets and the Zodiac took on different meanings and connotations. To the ancient Greeks the Planets were perceived as 'gods', who were the sons and daughters of Zeus, presiding over the world of mortals. And the 'Legend of Hercules', who is reputed to be half god and half man, tells the story of the Twelve Labours which Hercules performed to claim his own Divine Heritage and gain Immortality. And Hercules continued to grow in Strength as he steadfastly worked through, and assimilated, each 'Godlike

Virtue' associated with the Twelve Signs of the Zodiac. And although Hercules endured many death-defying trials, he was always thrown a life line by the 'gods', until he realised that the 'gods' are his own 'Consciousness', and that he was always the Rightful Ruler of his world.

And if we, like Hercules, have the Determination and Courage to devote all of our Attention to fulfilling our dreams and desires, while faithfully trusting in the Magical Light within us, regardless of appearances in our world, we too will Inherit the Kingdom of Heaven. And there is no difference between the 'Legend of Hercules' and the story that we are impressed with at our birth, which we believe is our only 'truth'; for every story is a unique combination of vibrations, reflected as a physical 'reality' in our world, which can be altered at the moment we change our Identity. For the world which now seems so 'physically real', is suspended on 'Nothing', and is formed entirely from the delusional stories devised by Humanity.

However, we must also appreciate that the people who first observed the course of the Planets in the night sky, and devised stories to explain their nature, knew that ultimately the Universe is animated by One Magical Life Force which is within and around everything. And that this Almighty Presence, which was regarded as the Self-Reproducing God-dess of Pure Magical Light of Celestial origin, would continue to Heal and Protect them forever. Therefore, these ancient people were not looking for, or expecting 'malefic' events to happen, since they had an abiding faith that nothing 'bad' could befall them while they were carrying out the Divine Will of the Beneficent God-dess on Earth. Hence, it is because of the anticipation of the majority of Humanity, who expect that something malevolent is about to happen, which causes the appearance of an undesirable situation to manifest in our world.

Nevertheless, the ancient Astrologers knew that while Prophesying or 'Speaking the Word' to affirm the 'Godlike Virtues' of a Leader, they were also defining their own destination (*destiny*); for when announcing the fruitful and successful outcome of the King's Reign, they were impressed with the same 'good vibrations' of the Prophecies they made. And the whole community also reaped the benefits, since they were One People, living in the same Kingdom. And by predicting the perfect out come to the King's Reign, the Astrologer was securing his own future, since he himself was part of the community, and he knew that he would be the recipient of his own predictions. Ancient Astrologers were also Physicians who were rewarded on results, and would not be paid for their services unless they predicted that the patient was now cured, which subsequently came to fruition. Hence, Astrologers truly believed in their own predictions, regardless of appearances in the world; for all ancient Astrologers were certain that the Perfect Virtues of the Zodiac Signs, and the Pure Consciousness of the Planets would be reflected on Earth, because it is the Divine Will of the God-dess.

Each Zodiac Sign now occupies 30 degrees of a 360-degree circle, although traditionally an Astrological chart was drawn as a square. And the Signs of Taurus (*the Bull*), Virgo (*the Virgin*), and Capricorn (*the Goat*), bestow the physical Virtues of Earth. The Signs of Cancer (*the Crab*), Scorpio (*the Scorpion*), and Pisces (*the Fish*), bestow the physical Virtues of Water. The Signs of Aries (*the Ram*), Leo (*the Lion*), and Sagittarius (*the Archer*), bestow the physical Virtues of Fire. While Gemini (*the Twins*), Libra (*the Scales*), and Aquarius (*the Water Bearer*), bestow the physical Virtues of Air. And each Zodiac Sign vibrates at a different frequency which is impressed as a memory on our DNA at the moment of our birth, and will remain in a constant Perfect State throughout life. However, it is the nature of the Planets, which represent our state of consciousness that cause the Perfect Virtues of the Zodiac to appear otherwise to our present limited perception.

Today, Astrology remains very popular and any individual who is curious about their own Astrological pattern can have a Horoscope cast, which is similar to a photograph taken of the Heavens at the moment we are born, if we know the accurate Date, Place and Time of birth. Consequently, it is alleged by Astrologers that when a material 'thing' is formed, or is born into the physical world, it shares the same qualities as the pattern evident in the Universe at that moment, revealed by the placement and relationship of the Planets in the Signs of the Zodiac on our birth chart. Hence, we continue to experience our story as our present Identity, which begins at the moment we take our first breath and became conscious of the world around us. And our story continues to develop according to where the Planets are now placed in the Heavens *(transits)*, and their relationship to the position of the Planets on our birth chart, known as the Aspects which measure the distance between Planets, and possible influence in our life.

However, aspects between Planets were not taken into consideration by ancient Astrologers in the same way they are now. For the pure energetic state of a Planet was judged according to its placement in the Signs of the Zodiac, which reveals the Material Element *(Fire, Earth, Air, and Water)* in which a Planet is situated. Thus, all Elements indicate different qualities in a person. Earth; Stability, Water; Coolness, Fire; Passion, and Air; Optimism. And while it is true that certain material Elements do complement each other, such as the Element of Fire combined with Air, and the Element of Earth combined with Water, the combination of Fire or

Air, with Earth or Water, are not naturally in a state of harmony, but they do offer us the opportunity to learn how to keep our bodily energies in balance, which will change our conscious perception of our 'self', and the world in which we live.

Ancient Astrologers also believed that the Seasons of the Year are represented by the Four Elements, which indicate when the Sun or a Planet would be at its most Magically Potent in the life of the Ruler, and whether the greatest triumphs of the Ruler would come through the Element of Earth, Water, Fire, or Air, or a combination of these. And when the potential Powers of the Elements, which are already inherent within us, are balanced in our Body, we improve our Magical proficiency to change our Self-Identity. For too much Earth and Water can cause our body to slow down and energy can become blocked, resulting in pain, discomfort or depression. And too much Fire and Air can cause us to become over heated or exited.

This viewpoint is similar to Chinese philosophy and the symbol of **Yin** and **Yang**, since **Yin** symbolises the slowing down of energy, while **Yang** symbolises a speeding up of energy, known as Chi, and neither are 'good' nor 'bad', they only signify different velocities of the same energy which must be kept in balance. And when a Planet is in a Zodiac Sign represented by Earth or Water, and another Planet is in a Zodiac Sign represented by Fire or Air, the Planets are said to be out of balance with each other. Hence, the energies of Planets in Earth or Water Signs may become overwhelmed by the Planets in Fire or Air Signs, causing the body to become agitated or aggressive. But it is also true that Fire and Air can be subdued by Earth and Water, causing a block in the free-flowing energy within the body. Thus, Planets placed furthest away from the Sun, which are Jupiter, Saturn, Uranus, Neptune, and Pluto, tend to influence the Moon, Mercury, Venus, and Mars, which are nearer to the Sun.

Nevertheless, when we are told by an Astrologer that our birth chart shows signs of adversity and misfortune, we tend to believe this is 'true'. But this prediction also harms the Astrologer, for while making such predictions they are inducing these adverse vibrations within themselves, which must, by the Law of Universe, be reflected in some way in the world of the Astrologer. For any prediction of misfortune contradicts the nature of the 'True Art of Astrology', which was only devised to reveal the Path of Humanity to our Divine Destination, and our liberation by inducing within us the Perfect Virtues of the Signs of the Zodiac. However, with the 'Fall of Humanity from Grace', when *Adam* perceived that something other than Pure Light existed, all people born ever since have inherited the same delusional, dual perception of 'reality'. Hence, the Pure Consciousness of the Planets is now considered to bestow both good and malefic qualities on people, which of course is in the 'Eye of the Beholder', and not in the nature of the Planets. And the plan, or story which is impressed as a vibration on our DNA at birth will continue to be experienced as our 'reality' throughout our lifetime, until we understand that it is our own limited perception of a situation which makes it 'real' in our world.

But since we are unaware of the Divine Nature of the Journey we are presently undertaking, we often react in anger and frustration toward our apparent situation, which can only be changed by altering our vibration to coincide with the story that we desire to be 'true'. For the Zodiac only consists of 'Perfect Godlike Virtues' and the Planets are 'Pure Divine Energies', made manifest in the Universe through our own conscious conceptions. And we are at liberty to experience our world in any way we choose; since the nature of the Zodiac and Planets only 'Impel' us to feel the pattern of our vibration at birth, but they do not 'Compel' us to do so.

Consequently, the Wisdom of Astrology has almost been lost through the mistaken perceptions of modern Astrologers and now bears no resemblance to its original conception; for like Kabbalah, Astrology has become more complex, and is now believed by many to play a sinister role in our lives, which we must quietly accept and endure. But we are always free to change our Identity, by knowing our own 'truth' within our Heart. Hence, when we look at our

Astrological birth chart we must appreciate the many possibilities which are bestowed upon us at birth, and not be diverted from our Divine Journey by being impressed with the stories of limitation we hear; for we now know that anything can be changed by inducing the sensation of different vibrations in our Heart and Body which will alter our perception of what appears to be 'real' in our world.

For the 'True Art of Astrology' reveals to us the 'Wisdom of the Stars' from whence our Celestial Ancestors came. And since the entire Magical Universe is within us, as we are in the Magical Universe, we are already impressed with the Perfect Virtues of the Zodiac and Pure Consciousness of the Planets at the moment we are born, which are just waiting to be revealed through us. For although we cannot alter the placement of the Planets at our birth, we can change the sensations we are now feeling by inducing the vibration of the Celestial Virtues within us by Speaking the Magical Word to change our Identity, and our perception of 'reality'.

Elements, Planets, Zodiac, and States of Consciousness

According to the *'Sefer Yetzirah'* the Seven Planets, and Twelve Signs of the Zodiac in Astrology, are formed by the Three Ethereal Elements, **Air, Water** and **Fire**, which are synonymous with the three Mother Letters, **AL, MAH & SHIN.** The Letter **MAH** signifies **Water** and Manifestation, and the Letter **SHIN** signifies **Fire** and Dissolution, while the Letter **AL** signifies **Air,** and is the Magical Breath in our Word which decides between the Manifestation or Dissolution of anything which appears, or disappears in our material world of shadows.

The Ethereal Elements of Air, Water and Fire are not represented in the practice of Astrology, for it was considered that although being the origin of creation, the Ethereal Elements are only possibilities which do not exist in material form. However, the Zodiac Signs, which represent the Material Elements of Fire, Earth, Air and Water, differ from the Ethereal Elements, since they vibrate at much denser frequencies which can be seen through the physical eye, with the exception of Air. But although physical Air is the most rarefied of all the Material Elements, and cannot normally be seen with the eye, it is not equivalent to the Ethereal Element of Air, for Ethereal Air has no physical substance. However, we know that the Material Element of Air consists of gaseous elements, which are adapted in the body to sustain life on the physical plane.

The Seven Heavenly Bodies that could be seen by ancient Astrologers without the aid of a telescope are **Saturn, Jupiter, Mars, Sun, Venus, Mercury,** and **Moon,** which are arranged in the *'Sefer Yetzirah'* according to their distance from Earth, and represent the Seven States of Consciousness which must be awakened within us to Reveal the Pure Magical Light of Heaven in our world.

BET - Saturn – *Conscious of Being Alive*

GAM - Jupiter – *Conscious of Pleasure or Pain*

DAL - Mars –*Conscious of Interaction with the physical world*

KAPH - Sun – *Conscious of Vital Energy flowing through our body*

PEY– Venus – *Conscious of the' Word' as our Prophecy*

RESH - Mercury – *Conscious of the Magical Universe*

TAW - Moon - *Conscious of our Wholeness in Paradise*

Nevertheless, according to the *'Sefer Zetzirah'*, the Hebrews considered the energy of the Seven Planets to be dual in nature, and that humans are influenced by the Planets for 'better' or 'worse'. Hence, the Planets are said to either enhance our conscious perception of Pure Light, or induce us to experience darkness and limitation, which is then seen all around us when our consciousness is not sufficiently developed to 'Know the Truth' of appearances. Thus, the concept of 'good' and 'evil' was established in the consciousness of Humanity, whereas before this story of duality was conceived, the Planets were considered to represent the Pure and Incorruptible Energy of the God-dess of Pure Light, who came from the Stars and gave birth to a Perfect Humanity. Hence, it is our own perception of 'good' and 'evil' which makes it appear so.

Dual Nature of Planets According to the *Sefer Yetzirah*

Saturn –BET – *Life or Death*

Jupiter – GAM – *Peace or Conflict*

Mars – DAL – *Wisdom or Ignorance*

Sun – KAPH – *Wealth or Poverty*

Venus –PEY – *Seed or Infertility*

Mercury – RESH – *Dominion or Oppression*

Moon – TAW – *Grace or Deception*

However, we must appreciate that to the ancient Phoenicians there was no choice between 'Light' and 'darkness', since to them only the Pure Light of the God-dess in Heaven exists. Thus, they saw everything in their world as now being how they desired it to be, and this was their habitual response to life's situations. Therefore, it is not a matter of choosing 'Light' over 'darkness', or 'good' before 'evil', but one of changing our present 'Identity' and our 'Perception of reality', by assimilating the vibrations of the Twelve Virtues of the Signs of the Zodiac, until we feel in our Heart and Body that everything in our world is already Perfect Now.

The Virtues of the Signs of the Zodiac in the *'Sefer Yetzirah'*

Aries (HEY) *Sight/Vision*

Taurus (VAV) *Hearing*

Gemini (ZAN) *Smell*

Cancer (HHETS) *Speech*

Leo (THET) *Taste*

Virgo (YAD) *Action (Touch)*

Libra (LAM) *Coition (Coalition)*

Scorpio (NUN) *Motion (Regeneration)*

Sagittarius (SIN) *Moderation of Anger (Temperance)*

Capricorn (AYIN) *Mirth (Light Heartedness)*

Aquarius (TSAD) *Thought (Conviction)*

Pisces (QUPH) *Sleep (Release)*

The Practice of Modern Astrology

Many modern Astrologers tend to judge a birth chart from the perspective that a person will experience situations in life as being either easy or hard, without regard to the original affirmative conception of Astrology, which was based on the Journey of a King to his Divine Destination. However, when the concept of 'good' and 'evil' was introduced to the once noble Art of Astrology, Astrologers from other Kingdoms began to make predictions of the downfall of a King or Leader of a neighbouring community; thus the battle of 'good' verses 'evil' commenced, not only with physical weapons, but also with the predictions of powerful magicians. Hence, Astrology and all Magical Arts were now viewed with suspicion and eventually forced underground, which made the practice of Astrology even more mysterious than it was to the original star gazers who only perceived the Perfect Virtues of the Signs of the Zodiac, and the Pure Energies bestowed by the Planets.

There are now several branches of Astrology, including Horary, *(judgement of the best hour to begin a new project)*, Synastry *(judgement of the possible relationship between people)*, and Mundane *(judgement of the fortunes of countries and leaders, and the outcomes of political dramas)*. The modern astrological chart now also incorporates Twelve Houses, or Mansions of the Soul, which show the areas of life where we might experience increase or demise at any particular moment in life. More recently the concept that the Zodiac Signs are said to represent different psychological characteristics, in which the placement of the Planets at our birth indicate whether our personality traits might manifest either in a 'positive' or 'negative' manner, to establish our Identity. And amazingly our birth chart actually does reveal the 'reality' that we will continue to experience throughout life, unless we intentionally choose to awaken dormant parts of our DNA, which will change our body at a cellular level, and alter the way in which we now perceive our 'reality'.

Therefore, if we are told by an Astrologer that the Planets at our birth are in a discordant relationship with each other, we should remember that all Planets and Zodiac Signs are Pure Unadulterated Energy; and Pure Energy cannot reproduce anything which is not in the same likeness as itself. And it is the discordant aspects which indicate where our 'Greatest Power' lies, and our opportunity to use this Power for the enhancement of self and Humanity. For the Magical Power inherent in the Planets is in no way malefic, so instead of feeling that the relationship of the Planets at our birth is something to be feared, or an excuse for our demise in the world, we should embrace our Astrological Pattern wholeheartedly and be thankful for the potential Energy that is inherent within us; for no 'individual' ever changed their world without first feeling a powerful urge to do so. And all 'easy aspects' on our birth chart, while often indicating a 'fortunate' life as a reward for past efforts, do not provide the impetus needed for growth and expansion.

The following lists show the interpretations that most modern Astrologers now attribute to the Planets and Signs of the Zodiac, which are still associated with the Letters of the Sacred Alphabet. However, the order of the Planets in modern Astrology differs from the story in the original version of the 'Sefer Yetzirah'.

Traditional Nature of the Planets

☉ **Sun KAPH** - represents the Expression of our innermost Self through our Imagination, Self-Identity, Fulfillment, Satisfaction, Accomplishment, Self-Importance, Honour, Dignity, Pride, Ambition, Self-Respect, and Command of our Vital Energy.

☽ **Moon TAV** - represents our Natural Response to Life's Situations, Fluctuations, Feminine Cycle, Receptiveness, Nurturing, Physical and Emotional Reactions, Domestic Harmony, Habitual Behaviour, Instinctive Feelings.

☿ **Mercury RESH** - is the Messenger through which we can Communicate between Heaven and Earth, as well as with our Inner Self and other people, Logical Thinking, Reasoning, Learning, Curiosity, Flexibility, Healing and 'Magic'

♀ **Venus PEY** - represents Appreciation for 'Art' in all forms, Relationship with Self and others, Femininity, Attractiveness, Fecundity, Love Affairs, Self-Indulgence, and Love of Nature.

♂ **Mars DAL** – signifies Determination, Activation, Courage, Circulation of Energy, Urge for Survival, Desire, Potency, Speed of Response, Self-Assertion, and all Cutting Instruments.

♃ Jupiter GAM - denotes Expansion, Preservation, Personal Development, Philanthropic Projects, Mercy, Charity, Spiritual Advancement, Growth, Self- Fulfillment, Faith, Financial Gain, Pleasure, and Graciousness.

♄ Saturn BET - represents Self-Discipline, Discernment, Structure, Endurance, Thrift, Concentrated Effort, Self-Imposed Restrictions and Limitations, Old Age, Duty, and Eventual Self-Re-Evaluation.

The Outer Planets which were discovered more recently are:

♅ Uranus AL - represents Revolutionary or Sudden Change of Circumstances, Inventiveness, Eccentricity, and Unusual Interests. (*Ethereal Element of Air which gives the opportunity for self-change*)

♆ Neptune MAH - is associated with Mystery, Intrigue, Mirages, Confusion, Delusion, Uncertainty, Unanswered Questions, and our Ultimate Enlightenment. (*Ethereal Element of Water which always reflects the true image of our self in the physical world of shadows*)

♇ Pluto SHIN - represents Extremes of Dissolution, Dissipation, Endings and Beginnings, Spiritual Awakenings, Regeneration and Re-Birth. (*The All-Consuming Ethereal Element of Fire which dissolves all misconceptions and gives birth to New Life*)

131

All Planets represent the Pure Energies which they were originally conceived to embody Within the Beginning. However, we cannot become aware of these Divine States of Consciousness unless we have the necessary equipment to experience these energies in our physical body. But when we are resonating with the vibrations of the Perfect Virtues of the Signs of the Zodiac, the cells in our body begin to attune to these frequencies, and we become conscious of new possibilities to which we were previously oblivious. Hence, if we are not living in our Paradise on Earth, we know it is because we are not yet resonating with our Ideal State in Heaven.

And although the three outer planets, Uranus, Neptune, and Pluto, are often blamed for the disruptions and difficult experiences that we might encounter life, and in the mundane affairs of Planet Earth, they actually herald the 'Awakening of Humanity' to a Whole New World of Possibility by changing our present perception of 'reality'. Therefore, we must induce new sensations within us, by changing our vibration through pronouncing the Letters of the Sacred Alphabet until these frequencies become impressed as memories on the DNA in our physical body. Hence, when we are no longer resonating at our old pattern of vibration, disruptive sensations, which are usually associated with lower frequencies of vibration, cannot be reflected through us and appear to become manifest as difficult situations in our world.

Traditional Virtues of the Signs of the Zodiac
(See page 136: 'Zealots of the Zodiac' Poem)

♈ **Aries HEY –**   **'I Am' -** 1st House – **Self-Identity**

Colour Red – **Assertively** - Ruled by Mars – Letter - **DAL**

Virtue: Sight - *to See the physical manifestation of our Inner Vision*

♉ **Taurus VAV -**   **'I Have'** - 2nd House – **Possessions**

Colour Red/Orange – **Possessively** - Ruled by Venus – Letter **PEY**

Virtue: Hearing– *to Hear only of our Possession of our Heart's Desire*

♊ **Gemini ZAN –**   **'I Think'** - 3rd House - **Communication**

Colour Orange – **Communicatively** - Ruled by Mercury – Letter **RESH**

Virtue: Smell–*to Focus on the Celebration of our Successful Communion*

♋ **Cancer HHETS -**   **'I Feel'** -   4th House - **Home**

Colour Orange/Yellow – **Sensitively** - Ruled by the Moon - Letter **TAV**

Virtue: Speech– *to Speak with Compassion and Empathy for 'All Life'*

♌ **Leo THET –**   **'I Create'** - 5th House – **Ingenuity**

Colour Yellow – **Creatively** - Ruled by the Sun - Letter **KAPH**

Virtue; Taste *– to Experience the Alchemical Transformation of our body*

♍ Virgo   YAD –   'I Analyse' - 6th House - **Healing/Service**

Colour Yellow/Green – **Methodically -** Ruled by Mercury - Letter **RESH**

Virtue: Action (Touch) - *to Feel our Present State of Perfect Health*

♎ Libra   LAM –   'I Balance' - 7th House- **Partnerships**

Colour Green – **Harmoniously** - Ruled by Venus - Letter **PEY**

Virtue: Coition (Coalition) - *to Be in Love with our Inner Spirit*

♏ Scorpio   NUN – 'I Regenerate' - 8th House –Transitions

Colour Green/Blue – **Passionately** - Ruled by Mars & Pluto

Letters **DAL** and **SHIN**

Virtue: Motion (Regeneration) - *to Narrate only stories of Miracles*

♐ Sagittarius SIN – 'I Adjust' -   9th House – **Philosophy**

Colour Blue – **Freely** - Ruled by Jupiter - Letter **GAM**

Virtue: Temperance of Anger – *to Forgive our Self, and All Others*

♑ Capricorn   AYIN – 'I Discern' 10th House – **Occupation**

Colour Blue/Violet – **Astutely** - Ruled by Saturn - Letter **AYIN**

Virtue: **Mirth –** *to See 'All Things' through the Eye of Discernment*

♒ **Aquarius TSAD – 'I Aspire'** 11th House –**Hopes & Dreams**

Colour Violet – **Aspiringly** - Ruled by Saturn and Uranus

Letters **AL and BET**

Virtue: **Thought** - *to Remain Faithful to our Divine Aspirations*

♓ **Pisces QUPH – 'I Realise'** 12th House –**Karma**

Colour Violet/Red- **Transcendentally** - Ruled by Jupiter and

Neptune - Letters **GAM** and **MAH**

Virtue: **Sleep (Release)** - *to 'Let Go' of delusions, and live in Paradise*

And how amazing it is when we consider that everyone in our world, including our parents, family, friends and partners, are all experiencing the same 'reality', seen from different perspectives, which we may not be aware of until we have eyes to see the 'truth', and ears to hear the 'significance' of the words that are being spoken. Thus, incredibly, we never form lasting relationships with people whose Astrological pattern, or Energetic Signature, does not correspond with our own in some way. Hence, we often see Astrological similarities between family members in their birth charts. And the following poem, 'Zealots of the Zodiac', will help us to recognise some of the personality characteristics which are prominent in people born when the Sun, or other Planets are in each of the Twelve Signs of the Zodiac.

Zealots of the Zodiac

♈ - Aries – I AM- Assertively

Impetuous, like a volcano wild and frenzied
I hurry to plight my troth with the world.
Unheeding, for the most part, of the dangers lurking
as headlong into life I am hurled.
To sow the seeds for future generations is the
Inspiration which spurs me onward to my goal.
And paying no attention to what appears before me,
I Elevate my Vision to Glorify my Soul.

♉ - Taurus – I Have - Possessively

I embrace the ideals of those who go before me
and with great patience I fashion them into form.
Through siege and tempest I cultivate with devotion,
holding on tight and riding the storm.
My eye beholds the beauty in every creature,
as I capture their essence in picture and in song.
And I'm steadfast in honouring my commitments;
remaining devoted to my Vows, all lifelong.

♊ - Gemini – I Think - Communicatively

I must converse to give my life meaning,

or pangs of boredom would surely take their toll.

An agile mind that needs constant stimulation,

and dextrous fingers never ceasing in their goal.

I have no time for those who plod and dawdle,

as if tomorrow were soon enough to act.

But when focusing in on the Magical Light within me,

I know Success will be the result this Mystical Act.

♋ - Cancer – I Feel - Sensitively

I Secure the doors and batten down the hatches

to ensure the Protection and Preservation of my spawn,

and I gather up supplies of every food and potion

in readiness for winter, though the season is still warm.

I embody the emotions of all those who are around me,

and Speak Words of Compassion for everyone.

For I Feel an inner need to nurture everything in nature;

knowing the 'Divine Essence within All Life', is One.

♌ - Leo – I Inspire - Creatively

Oh, glorious Sun, who graciously shines upon me,

and whose golden rays keep me glad and in good health.

I am the 'King' who is destined to Rule with you, and

to Transform this Earth into a Paradise of Wealth.

Hence, to this end my Heart is strong and resolute, as I

Taste the Transmuting Power of Alchemy on my Tongue.

So, chastise me not for my keen and ardent fervour;

for I overflow with the Vibrant Spirit of the Sun.

♍ - Virgo – I Analyse - Methodically

At all times I need to attain perfection

in everything which I endeavour to do.

And no matter how precise the task or duty

I struggle and strive until I see it through.

Thus, all affairs to do with health and hygiene

are inspirations to my meticulously tidy mind.

But when Touched with the Hand of Restoration,

my World is Healed of imperfections of all kind.

♎ - Libra – I Balance - Harmoniously

I hold the Scales of Justice and of reason

with which the facts I balance and I weigh.

I'll consider all the evidence before me,

and be absorbed with everything you say.

My usual manner, although pleasant and endearing,

may not reach a final decision of any kind,

until in Coalition with the Divine Spirit within me,

my Love of Justice will Illuminate my mind.

♏ - Scorpio – I Regenerate – Passionately

My earnest passions they run so very deeply

that I often find it difficult to detach.

I keep all secrets under lock and key inside me

and my sense of intrigue is virtually unmatched.

When I fall in love, it is with great intensity,

and every Motion is devoted to generating my ideal.

But I know my world is only the reflection of the stories

which I continue to Narrate, and now believe are 'real'.

♐ - Sagittarius – I Adjust - Freely

The rightful liberty to roam free and unencumbered
is more precious to me than any words can say.
Thus, to explore the Universe and its many wonders
is the desire which impels me to go my own way.
I recount the tales of my many intriguing adventures,
while modifying their endings, just for fun.
And if at times I may seem distant or preoccupied,
it is because I am feeling the urge to follow the Sun.

♑ - Capricorn – I Discern - Astutely

I always look before I leap into the action
so that I know beyond all doubt just where I'll land.
I act cool and unperturbed in the face of danger
and won't gamble with a less than certain hand.
I have panache when it comes to brass and business,
never missing opportunities as they arise.
And I Observe all appearances with amusement;
for they are only shadows which deceive my eyes.

.

♒ - Aquarius - I Aspire - Detachedly

Being totally independent and original,

although some would say I'm really just perverse,

I will lead a revolution against convention,

knowing that all appearances can be reversed.

And new gadgets, devices, and inventions

draw my interest, and so I hold them in esteem.

But my Thoughts reveal a Vision for Humanity,

and for Peace on Planet Earth, 'I Have A Dream'.

♓ - Pisces - I Release – Transcendentally

Although I overflow with human kindness,

I often lack resolve to see things through.

And just how my disposition flows or fluctuates,

depends on if I'm seeing Red, or feeling Blue.

From deep within I feel a need to renounce this world,

to break free from the delusionary chains which bind,

Thus, Crossing Over into Paradise with my Inner Spirit,

I Now Sleep Peacefully in Body, Soul and Mind.

These light-hearted descriptions of the various character traits associated with the Zodiac Signs are quite amusing, and even revealing, but we must remember that Astrology was originally devised to guide us through the 'Circle of Life' by way of our own 'Self-Revelation'. Therefore, we must 'let go of', or relinquish our human insecurities, and allow the Pure Conscious of the Planets to express the Perfect Virtues of the Zodiac through us, until the 'Ancient Wisdom' of our Celestial Ancestors is manifest on Earth.

Today Western Astrology has become increasingly misunderstood and misinterpreted since its original conception. For what began as a way of revealing Paradise on Earth, or to assess the Perfect Virtues and Pure Consciousness of a future King, has now developed into a fortune telling device which humans believe controls their fate. But while it is true that we are each influenced by the placement of the Planets in the Zodiac at the moment of our birth, most modern astrologers interpret a birth chart as having both 'good' and 'malefic' connotations, which are suggested to be the cause of any inharmonious traits of character, or difficult experiences that we might encounter in life; thereby predicting a possible undesirable outcome to the story of our destiny. However, our Divine Heritage is already assured Within the Beginning when the potential for all life was conceived to be Perfect, even though many Astrologers now proclaim that the Pure Magical Life Force can, and actually does re-produce something other than Its 'Perfect Reflection'. And this is because all humans born since Adam are unable to Perceive the Perfection of the Magical Universe, now having been impressed with the Sharp Seeds of 'shame' and 'guilt'. But once we become conscious of our Divine Magical Inheritance as a child of the Celestial God-dess of Pure Light, which remains unchanged throughout Eternity, our world will be miraculously transformed at the moment we choose to perceive our self in this way. For we are not enslaved by the Stars, and each of us is in charge of our own destiny; therefore, the fault, if any, is not in the Stars, but in our habitual responses to life's situations. However, the Wisdom of Kabbalah and Astrology, which was taught by Abraham, to show us the Way to 'create' a Paradise on Earth, will continue to form our world in our own Image, if we only have eyes to see clearly.

Hence, our birth chart reveals our own unique plan, or the Virtues that we inherited at birth, which are memories impressed as a pattern on our DNA. But it all depends on how we are now feeling and our perception and reaction to the events which appear to be happening in our world which forms our Self-Identity, and reveals our destiny. For when we feel that we are on a Spiritual Journey to our Divine Destination, accompanied by our Soul Mate that is the Pure Essence of the Sun, or Celestial Star Seed Which Dwells Within Us, we will continue to live in Paradise of Earth. But if we believe we are a victim of fate, and have no control over our destiny, we will continue to live in a world of shadows; still searching in vain for the 'Pure Light' which is already inherent within us. However, we cannot change our present situation until we feel the sensation in our Heart and Body of our fulfilled desired, and consciously witness this 'State of Being' to now be our 'truth' in the world.

Therefore, we cannot live with one foot in Heaven, while every now and again slipping back into our old identity; for Magic only happens when we are absolutely convinced of who we are, and we continually remain in this Elevated State of Consciousness. Thus, our birth chart, when properly understood, can help us to devise new stories through which we can express the Perfect Virtues of the Zodiac and Pure Consciousness of the Planets, by pronouncing the resonant sounds associated with the Letters of the Sacred Alphabet. And our Journey through the Zodiac will continue until we have become the 'Master of our own Destiny', now knowing that the world in which we live, and see all around us, is only the reflection of our own deluded perception. However, this is not to say that the physical world is not 'real', since it reveals the pattern of vibration which is presently impressed on our DNA, and is our only way of knowing who we believe our self to be. But once we know that this pattern is only a memory of what has already been felt within us, we will no longer react to this world in the same way we once did.

However, if we believe that we were born at an unfortunate moment in time when the Planets were in an inharmonious relationship with each other, we must change this assumption; since the Planets and Zodiac Signs were declared to be Perfectly Functioning Within the beginning, and therefore, cannot be functioning imperfectly now. Hence, it is the present deluded perception of Humanity which causes 'reality' to appear otherwise. For all stories and predictions, when spoken with intention, tend to come to fruition; not because it is 'Written in the Stars, but because of the Magical Power inherent in our Feelings and our Words.

But every planetary configuration on our birth chart gives us the opportunity for Growth and Expansion, once we understand that we are always free to feel the sensation of any vibration that we choose, regardless of how we might be feeling right now. Hence, we must change the vibrations that we are now experiencing by speaking the Letters of the Sacred Alphabet, which are associated with the Zodiac Signs, and Planets, to induce only benign sensations within us; which is the antidote to any supposed 'hard aspect' on our birth chart. And if we alter any adverse sensation that we might now be feeling, these vibrations cannot be reflected through us, and appear as solid physical particles in our world.

The 'Story of Creation', Kabbalah and Astrology are all stories devised by ancient Mesopotamian people, which are based on the Sacred Phoenician Alphabet. But there is no evidence to suggest that the Phoenicians themselves practiced Kabbalah and Astrology in the same way as the surrounding communities; since the early Phoenicians lived in an egalitarian society without any leader, and knew that the Whole of Humanity is on a Sacred Journey to our Divine Destination together. Hence, no one person was more important than another in Phoenician Society. Nevertheless, since the Phoenicians embarked on many long sea voyages, we can assume they used the Stars to navigate between destinations. And possibly, because the Phoenicians regarded every sea voyage as a Pilgrimage in Honour of the Self-Reproducing Mother God-dess of Pure Light, they were always successful while trading their much sort after goods; which included the famous 'Tyrian Purple Dye' that was produced by the Phoenicians from the shells of molluscs, and traded throughout the Mediterranean and far beyond.

Thus, we know that the use of colour was very important to the Phoenician way of life, for colour in all its hues, shades, and tones signified the Presence of the Power of the Beneficent Mother God-dess of Pure Magical Light on Earth, especially when seen in the form of a Colourful Rainbow surrounding the Earth.

The Meaning of Colour Vibrations

The Birth Chart is our own personal Colour Wheel, which is seen on the front cover of this book, and indicates how we might experience our own 'Life Story'; since everything in the Universe is Vital Energy vibrating at various frequencies and velocities, which appear to our eyes to be solid and static. Visible light ranges from red (longest wavelength) through to violet (shortest wavelength) which produce the vibrations that we now feel are 'real' within us. The electromagnetic radiation which is visibly perceivable as colour to the normal human eye, ranges from red, with a frequency of 400 terahertz, to violet, with a frequency of 790 terahertz, and has wavelengths between 750 nanometres and 380 nanometres respectively. And since our body is a combination of vibrating energies, when we see or wear a particular colour it causes our body to resonate at the same frequency, which is then revealed in our world as a physical manifestation.

This phenomenon was appreciated by the Phoenicians who chose to wear a 'Metaphorical Robe' in the same colour, or frequency of vibration they desired to induce in their body. For when wearing a Robe of a specific colour it transforms the sensation which we are presently feeling within us, until we feel this new vibration, which is then reflected as a 'reality' in our world. The ancient Phoenicians were also renowned for manufacturing 'Tyrian Purple Dye', which represents the Power of Sovereignty, since it was the colour of the robes worn by Emperors and Kings as a sign of their Authority and Divine Right to Rule.

Thus, when we feel the vibration of **Red,** which is synonymous with **DAL, Mars,** and **HEY, Aries,** we become Animated, Extrovert, Virile, Accelerated, Passionate, Driven, Courageous, Intentional, Motivated, Energised, Vigorous, Expectant, and Elevated.

When we experience the vibration of **Orange,** which is synonymous with **ZAN, Gemini,** and **RESH, Mercury,** we become Buoyant, Communicative, Sociable, Happy, Joyful, Enthusiastic, Gregarious, Charismatic, Focused, Clear Minded, and Magical.

When we feel the vibration of **Yellow,** which is synonymous with **THET, Leo, and KAPH, Sun,** we become Spirited Alchemists, Commanding, Distinguished, Regal, Influential, Radiant, Alert, Vital, Confident, Creative, Wealthy, Prosperous, Abundant, Imaginative, Inventive, and Transformed. Pale Yellow is often associated with **Uranus** and unpredictability and change.

When we experience the vibration of **Green,** which is synonymous with **LAM, Libra** and **PEY, Venus,** we feel Loved, Loving, In Love, Thankful, Grateful, Harmonious, Balanced, Open Hearted, Healed,

Guided, Fruitful, Fertile, Regenerated, Rejuvenated, Prophetic, Artistic, and Miraculous.

When we experience the vibration of **Blue,** which is synonymous with **GAM, Jupiter, SIN, Sagittarius, and MAH, Ethereal Element of Water** and **Neptune,** we Feel Calm, Peaceful, Reflective, Compassionate, Forgiving, Forgiven, Contented, Inspired, Blessed, Benevolent, Loyal, Tranquil, Serene, and Relaxed.

And when we feel the vibration of **Violet,** which is synonymous with **TSAD, Aquarius,** and **TAV, Moon,** we become Dignified, Majestic, Sincere, Faithful, Devoted, Committed, Resolute, Convinced, Certain, Knowing, Trusting, Magically Adept, Wise, Expansive, Whole, Complete, Triumphant, and Enlightened.

Letters that are a combination of colours incorporate the qualities of both colours, and include: *Red/Orange* **VAV, Taurus;** *Orange/Yellow* **HHETS, Cancer;** *Yellow/Green,* **YAD, Virgo;** *Green/Blue,* **NUN, Scorpio;** *Blue/Violet,* **AIYN, Capricorn;** *Violet /Red,* **QUPH, Pisces,** and **SHIN, Ethereal Element of Fire**, and **Pluto.** The colour *Black,* represents **BET** and **Saturn,** which absorbs all colours, *and Pure White,* is represented by **AL,** and **Ethereal Element of Air**, which reflects all colours. And when we pronounce words in a resounding tone of voice, with Intention, a range of colourful vibrations are induced in the cells of our body. Thus, being in command of the sensations we choose to feel will alter how we experience and perceive our world. For we are all artists, selecting the colours with which we will paint the picture of our own Life Story. But we will never become 'Masters of our Craft', until we surrender to the Magic of the 'Divine Inner Artist', and together we will create miraculous masterpieces in our world. The list below shows how we can change our present circumstances by inducing different colourful vibrations in our body when we Speak each Sacred Letter with Resonance, Feeling, and Intention

To Alter our Present Perception with Colourful Vibrations
Change Self-Identity: AL, *Pure White;* **MEM,** *Blue;* **SHIN,** *Violet/Red*
To Induce Courage: DAL; *Red;* **HEY,** *Red;* **NUN,** *Green/Blue*
Remove Addictions: GAM, *Blue,* **SIN,** *Blue;* **QUPH,** *Violet/Red*
Improve Health: ZAN, *Orange;* **YAD,** *Yellow/Green;* **RESH,** *Orange*
Financial Assistance: GAM *Blue;* **THET,** *Yellow;* **KAPH,** *Yellow*
To Find True Love: VAV, *Red/Orange;* **LAM,** *Green;* **PEY,** *Green*
Wisdom and Insight: AL, *Pure White;* **BET,** *Blue/Violet;* **AYIN,** *Blue/Violet*
To Connect with our Celestial Ancestors: HHETS, *Orange/Yellow;*
TSAD, *Violet;* **TAV,** *Violet.*

Healing with Colourful Words

The Phoenicians regarded the Universe as a Magic Circle of Colour reflected in the Water in the womb of the God-dess, which is the place where we live, and play the 'Game of Life'. And the only Rule of the Game is that we must first experience the sensation of being who we desire to be, before we can become this person in our world. Hence, the Phoenicians knew that by experiencing the Pure White Light at the Silent Centre of our 'Magic Circle, any dream or desire can come to fruition; for Pure Light contains the frequencies of all colours. And retreating from the material world into the Silence of the Heart, everything which once appeared to be 'real' was now in a 'State' of Nothingness', as it is Within the Beginning. And devising a story they desired to be 'true', the Phoenicians began to feel their fulfilled desire was already a 'reality'.

While wearing a 'Metaphorical Robe of Many Colours', which changed appearance according to the vibration of colour the Phoenicians desired to experience, they gave thanks for the Magical Transformation which had already taken place within them. Then continuing to wear this Robe in the colour they intended to induce in their body, their Miraculous Transformation became evident in the world. For as each Sacred Letter is Spoken with resonance, it alters the sensation we feel in our body, until we become conscious of a new 'Identity'. And once we are familiar with the 'Process of

Self-Creation' now taking place within us, we will instantly induce the sensation of any fulfilled desire within us through our Word; since we are essentially beings of Pure White Light who exist is a 'Sea of Nothingness', and all the Splendour of the Rainbow is already inherent within us, just waiting to be expressed in our world. Hence when we pronounce the Letters of the Sacred Alphabet with Intention, and feel the vibration of the associated colour within us, we can change any misconception, or physical appearance. Since what we experience and see in our world is only the reflection of the vibration we now feel is 'real' in our body.

All words have power, which can alter the colourful vibration that we are feeling within us, through our own 'Intention'. And since everything in our world is connected in the Pure Magical Light, when someone appears to be in need of healing, we must realise that what we are seeing is the reflection of a colour, or vibration that we are resonating with our self. Therefore, we can alter the appearance of another person, not by acknowledging their present apparent condition, but by changing the 'lame man' within our self. For knowing that all which exists is 'Pure White Light', which is refracted through the prism of our own personal understanding, we can 'Heal the Whole World' when we forgive our own misconceptions, and change our self. And when we speak the 'Word of Healing' for our self, or another person, and identify with the sensation of 'Perfect Health', the appearance of the person, and the whole world will change accordingly. But when we continue to feel someone is in need of healing for any conceivable condition, then we deny our Divine Heritage, and our distorted perception of 'reality' continues to appear as an imperfection in our world.

For when we breathe in Pure Light, and allow the Light to circulate throughout our body, until we experience it changing colour in accordance with the vibration of the Word we have spoken, our body begins to resonate at a different frequency. Thus, when we speak the Letter **YAD (Y)**, which is associated with the colour Yellow/Green, we induce the sensation of Healing throughout our body and beyond; for our body does not end at our skin, but continues in an Unseen Ethereal Form throughout the entire Universe. And once we realise that we are Everywhere, and Everyone is part of our self, we will understand why people are healed once we change our own vibration. However, we never consider specific conditions, since all dis-ease is the same vital energy appearing to manifest in various forms, and to different degrees, but concentrate instead on the Healing Sensation of Pure White Light and the vibration of Colour now flowing through our entire body, and far beyond. For 'everything' is conceived Perfect Within the Beginning, and it is the limited perception of 'Humanity' which makes it appear otherwise.

153

Therefore, when we tell the story of a 'Miraculous Healing', we are declaring that the State of Perfection which is conceived to be 'True' Within the Beginning is still 'true' now, if only we have eyes to see clearly. Hence, when we 'Speak the Word of Healing' for our self, or another person, we must change our perception of 'reality', until our prophecy appears as an observable 'fact' in our world.

According to Kabbalists we can also consider the areas of the Mouth that are used when forming 'Healing Words'; for it is the ability of the mouth to speak which is the power that affects our personal environment, and our whole world. And each Sacred Letter corresponds to an area of the Mouth that is touched by the Tongue when a Letter or Word is spoken, will help focus our attention on the resonance of that Word, and bring to fruition our desired Intention. For the Mouth is the feminine aspect of the androgynous God-dess, which is the 'Womb of Creation', and the Tongue is the masculine attribute of the God-dess, or the phallus which impregnates the Womb with the conception of new life. And each area of the Mouth invokes a different vibration which Sows the Seeds of our desired Intention in the cells of our body.

For 'Speaking' is an 'Art', as well as a 'Science', that when mastered will bring about the appearance of a Whole New World before us. And our 'Reality' is formed by the colourful vibrations of the

Letters which form the Words that we speak. Therefore, since the Sacred Letters were devised by the Phoenicians to Sow the Seeds of only Benign Sensations in our Heart and Body, the Sacred Letters cannot be used to form Words with malefic connotations; hence, it is our own misguided understanding of the power inherent in Words, and our intention which makes our words now appear so.

Vibrations Produced in the Mouth by the Sacred Letters

Mouth - Passive Empty Womb – Silence

AL,   HEY,   HHETS (*guttural cH*) , **AYIN** (*Oyin*)
Guttural - Throat – Seed of Pure Sensation
(*produced in the throat and not touching the Mouth*)

GAM,   YAD,   KAPH (*Kaf*),   **QUPH** (*kof*)
Palatal – Roof of Mouth – Seed of Inspiration

DAL,   THET (*Tet*),   **LAM,   NUN** (*Noon*),   **TAW** (*Tov*)
Lingual – Tip of Tongue – Seed of Activation

ZAN, (*Zain*) **SIN,   TSAD,   RESH,   SHIN** (*Sheen*)
Dental - Teeth – Seed of Integration

BET (*Beit*),   **VAV** (*Vov*),   **MAH or MEM,   PEY**
Labial - Lips – Seed of Manifestation
(*Known as the Kiss of the Goddess*)

The Mouth is a Silent, Empty Vessel until impregnated with the Word which is formed by the placement of the Tongue in the Mouth. And it is the pronunciation of the Spoken Sacred Letters in the five areas of the Mouth which Unite Heaven and Earth and perpetuate the cycle of Self-Creation.

Guttural - Throat – Sensation

AL–*To Feel Empowered by the Presence of Pure Magical Light*

HEY – *To Breathe in Pure Light, and See our Vision of Perfection*

HHETS *(guttural cH) – To Preserve and Protect the Sanctity of All Life*

AYIN *(Oyin) – To Expand our Perception of 'Reality'*

Roof of Mouth - Palate – Inspiration

GAM – *To Reflect on the Calm Sensation of Paradise on Earth*

YAD - *To Experience Holistic Healing from Within*

KAPH *(Kaf) – To Energise our body by the Power of Our Word*

QUPH *(Kof) – To Cross Over into a New Dimension*

Lingual - Tongue - Activation

DAL – *To Establish the 'Reality' of our Dream in our world*

THET *(Tet) - To Change our Perception of 'Self' and our 'Reality'*

LAM – *To Be in Love with Our Divine Inner Spirit*

NUN *(Noon) To Continue to Nourish through the stories we tell*

TAW *(Tov)– To Witness the Completeness of our Magical Universe*

Dental - Teeth – Integration

ZAN *(Zain) - To Reap the Seeds of our Certain Success*

SIN– *To Forgive all Misconceptions and Delusional Stories*

TSAD – *To Strengthen Resolve and Trust in the Power of Inner Light*

RESH – *To Surrender to the Magic of our Divine Inheritance*

SHIN *(Sheen)* – *To Arise Transformed into a New State of Being*

Labial - Lips – 'The Kiss of the Goddess' - Manifestation

BET *(Beit) - To Embody the Light of our Celestial Ancestors*

VAV – *To Know that Heaven and Earth is always United within us*

MAH– *To Become One with Our Desired Self- Reflection*

PEY– *To Speak only of Magical Stories with Miraculous Endings*

For all Words have the Power to produce *Miraculous Endings* to our Stories, and it is the limited 'knowledge' and 'misunderstandings' of Humanity which often make the endings of our stories appear otherwise. But the more we identify with the resonant sounds of the Sacred Words that we are speaking, the greater our ability to perform 'Magical Acts' will become; for we are the originator and narrator of our own Life Story, and all Miracles which appear to manifest in our world must come through us. This brings us to the 'Story of the Tarot' which can reveal many aspects of our Life Story that we are presently experiencing, but, as we know, our Life Story can be changed, once we perceive our 'reality' in a New Light.

The Origins of the Tarot

Although the Tarot was not originally based on the Symbols of the Sacred Alphabet, similar to Kabbalah and Astrology, Tarot is a system which guides us through an Inner Journey of Self-Discovery by the Symbolism of the Cards. The Twenty-Two Major Arcane Cards of the Tarot were allegedly developed in Egypt, and reveal the 'Fool', or Innocent person, starting out on a Journey to his Divine Destination. However, looking at the different religious beliefs and customs of Ancient Egypt, the Tarot may have originally been the instructions to guide a Pharaoh through the Underworld to the Afterlife, where he would Rule forever with the Sun. For a Pharaoh was seen to be 'Innocent' or without fault, and having the Divine Right to Rule his Kingdom; since it was considered that he was descended from the Star People of Sirius. And it is alleged by many philosophers and historians that these 'god like people', who were described as 'Beings of Pure Light with Knowledge of Magic and Healing', came to Earth long ago, and founded the fabled Atlantis. Thus, a Pharaoh, by declaring himself to be the descendant of these 'Miraculous Beings', established himself as a Divine Ruler on Earth.

The Three Stars of Sirius, which are regarded as female, may be synonymous with the Three Mother Letters of the Sacred Alphabet. Since the Star Sirius A, known as the Dog Star, is the brightest star in the Sky, which may equate with the Light of the Letter **AL** *(Ethereal Element of Air)*. And Sirius B, which is a dwarf star that exerts an enormous gravitational pull on the other stars around it, may correspond with the Letter **MAH** *(Ethereal Element of Water)*. While Sirius C, which was not discovered until much later, since it is always shifting in and out of sight, and may be synonymous with the **Letter SHIN** *(Ethereal Element of Fire)*. Thus, the Three Sacred Mother Letters could correspond to the **'Fool'** *(AL)*, the **'Hanged Man'** *(MEM)*, and **'Judgement'** *(SHIN)* in Tarot; signifying that we are **'Innocent'**, or **Unaware**, until we **Reverse** our perception of 'reality' and realise that we are the **Judge** of our self, and our world.

And as we know, it was of vital importance to keep the body in perfect condition by embalming the remains of a Pharaoh after his apparent death in this world, to ensure that he could return to his body and continue to Rule on Earth. For without a physical body with which to feel the sensation of 'Being Alive', it was thought that a Pharaoh's Soul would be lost for eternity. Therefore, to the Egyptians, having a body to experience one's own 'Identity' was paramount in Egyptian Ideology, and to the Practice of Egyptian Magic. However, while a Pharaoh was convinced that his Spirit would reincarnate into his old body, the people from surrounding communities believed that the physical body of a King would either be transformed into 'Pure Light' as he became merged with his

Inner Spirit, or that the Spirit of a King after death would reincarnate into a new body to experience himself again. Therefore, there was no need to preserve the old body after death; for it was accepted that whatever, or whoever we consciously identify our self with at the moment of our apparent death, will define the body, and the life that we will experience in our next incarnation.

The Tarot today represents everyone's Divine Journey through Life, starting out as the 'Fool', believing this world of shadows is our only 'reality', and ending our Journey after being re-born into a new life, represented by the Tarot Card 'The World'. And the Major Arcane when laid in a circle reveals the Process of Self-Development which takes place within us during our Journey to our Divine Destination. For we start out on our Journey through Life in a certain place, and arrive back at the same place where we started, but now 'having an enhanced understanding of our 'reality', since the only place there is 'Here' and 'Now'. Hence, the only way to become 'Enlightened' is by consciously inhabiting a physical body, in which we can experience being the person who we now desire to be. Thus, eventually, we will become sufficiently conscious to instantly produce a different physical body whenever one is needed, once we know that it is our own 'Self-Identity' that is the 'Key which unlocks the Magical Power of Self-Reproduction which is already inherent within us at birth.

160

The Tarot later became associated with Kabbalah, which is possibly when each of the Twenty-Two pictographs were given a numerical value, since there is no evidence to suggest that numbers were ascribed to the original Tarot. For similar to the Mystical Kabbalah and the Art of Astrology, the Tarot was not a regimented system, but a Spiritual Path which allows us to devise our own Life Story; since our Journey from Embryo to Enlightenment depends on our choices which we are free to change at any moment. Thus, the numbers which now appear on Tarot Cards, begin at Zero, representing 'the 'Fool' and the State of Nothingness' and the Letter **AL**, and end at number Twenty-One, which is the climax of our Journey, signified by the 'Universe' or 'World', and the Letter **TAV**. This final card indicates our attainment in our World, while in partnership with our Celestial Inner Spirit, or Sun. And subsequently, the Tarot was introduced to Europe as a card game, probably by travelling Gypsies (*Egyptians*), and the fifty-six cards of the Minor Arcane were later added to the Twenty-Two Major Arcane Cards, making a total of seventy-eight cards in all, and became a devise used to predict fortunes.

Today there are many versions of the Tarot which place the order of the Major Arcane Cards in different positions, that can be quite confusing to the student, but serves to preserve the secrecy of their true significance. Of course, the changing order of the Cards might also suggest that our Journey to our Divine Destination is not yet 'set in stone' and that we are always free to formulate the finer details of our Journey. Hence, when a Tarot reader lays the Cards on behalf of a client, they are alleged to reveal the present direction that the client is headed, which may either enhance and speed up the Journey, or delay their arrival at their desired destination. If the Tarot reader is sufficiently rehearsed in the significance of the Cards, they are then able to 'predict' the events or situations that the client could possibly encounter while on their Journey. However, a Tarot reader should always point out to the client that we have free will, and therefore our Life Story can always be altered at any moment. But if the client accepts what they have been told, and has felt the vibration of this prediction as a sensation in their body, then it will become a 'reality' in the world.

Nevertheless, we should also remember that the Tarot Cards are not founded on the Letters of Sacred Phoenician Alphabet which were devised to only induce beneficent sensations in a person, which is not the case with many Tarot readings. And when a client is told that they may experience an undesirable outcome to their situation, it forms a vibration in the body of both the reader and the client. And both then become conscious of this sensation within the cells of their body. Therefore, we must be careful when we make or hear predictions, that we are not impressed with the vibration of undesirable stories. However, when we are in Command of the Sensations that we allow to flow through our body, we are in control of our own fate, and have no need for a fortune teller to predict the outcome of our Journey; since our Divine Destination (*destiny*) is already assured 'Within the Beginning', and therefore we know it must come to fruition.

The following list gives a brief interpretation of the Twenty-Two Major Arcane Cards of the Tarot, which are a guideline to help students become more familiar with the traditional meanings ascribed the Tarot Cards. But, as with all methods of Self-Development, each student must find the answer to their questions within their own Heart; for the Journey to our Divine Destination is different for every individual. The names of the Tarot Cards below are placed in the order which is recommended by most Tarot readers. However, they do not follow the same sequence as the original Letters of the Sacred Phoenician Alphabet, and it is up to each student to come to their own conclusion on this matter.

The order in which the Tarot Cards would appear if they were in correspondence with the Sacred Letters, is shown in 'Twenty-Two Steps to the Process of Self-Creation' on page 169, and differs from the order of the Cards as depicted by modern Tarot Readers.

Twenty-Two Major Arcane Cards of the Tarot
(in the sequence they appear today)

0 – Fool –often associated with Innocence, Originality, Journey, Quest, Opportunity, Eccentricity and Impulsive Action, Beginning of a New Phase of Life.

1 – Magician –often associated with Power, Initiative, Skills, Dexterity, Subtlety, Channelling Knowledge, and Occult Wisdom of the Magical Arts.

2 – High Priestess – often associated with Duality, Fluctuation, Secrets, Hidden Things, Mystery, Casting Spells, Feminine Power, Lunar Inspiration, and Dreams.

3 – Empress –often associated with Nature, Fecundity, Birth, Motherhood, Fruitfulness, Beauty, Luxury, Pleasure, Abundance, and Sensuality.

4 – Emperor –often associated with Patriarchy, Self-Definition, Stability, Reason, Power, Orthodoxy, Ambition, Authority, and Master of all he Surveys.

5 – Hierophant – often associated with Tradition, Morality, Devotion, Teaching, Inspiration, Alliance, Commitment, Loyalty, and Inner Guidance.

6 – Lovers – often associated with Agreement, Self-Knowledge, Choices, Clarification, Communication, Celebration, Marriage, and Consummation.

7 – Chariot –often associated with Control over Nature, Maturity, Experience, Self-Development, Triumph, Victory, through the Regulation of Magical Forces.

8 – Strength – often associated with Courage, Fortitude, Life-Force, Endurance, Creativity, Self-Control, Lust for Life, Metaphysical Quests.

9 – Hermit –often associated with, Imagination, Wisdom, Prudence, Inner Teaching, Self- Guidance, Introspection.

10 – Wheel of Fortune – often associated with Destiny, Good Fortune, Change of Perception, New Opportunities.

11 – Justice – often associated with the satisfactory outcome of Mundane Issues and Legal Affairs, and Lawsuits, Decisions.

12 – Hanged Man – often associated with Reversals, Rites of Passage, Unconventionality, Mysticism, Martyrdom, Wisdom in Spiritual Matters,

13 – Death – often associated with Transitions, Elimination, Intense Experiences, Sudden Changes, Endings, New Beginnings.

14 – Temperance – often associated with Forgiveness, Adaptation, Blending, Management, Skilfulness Life-Force, Renewal, Blending, Creative Solutions.

15 – Devil – often associated with Temptation, Discernment, Defective Perception, Self-Imposed Suffering, Bondage, Ego, Materialism.

16 – The Lightning Struck Tower – often associated with Potency, Ambition, Break up of Structures, Release of Energy, Bolt of Inspiration, Spiritual Realisation.

17 – Star –often associated with Insight, Hope, Inner Light, Recognition, Altruistic Impulses, Faith, Following our own Star, Absolute Conviction of our own Self-Identity.

18 – Moon – often associated with Self-Deception, a Leap of Faith into the Unknown, Voluntary Change, Shape Shifting, Deep Cellular Change, Evolution, Release from Misconceptions.

19 – Sun – often associated with Gain, Wealth, being Energised by the Life-Giving Rays of the Sun, Realisation of Goals, New Insight, Recognition for Accomplishments, Enlightenment.

20– Judgement – often associated with Freedom, Awakening, Liberty, Self-Judgement, Dissolution, Metamorphosis, and Re-Birth.

21 – Universe – often associated with Infinite Potential, Change in Circumstances, Completion, Self- Realisation, Synthesis, Unification of All Elements, Self-Rule, and Enlightenment.

Every Tarot reader has their own opinion of which Sacred Letter is assigned to each Tarot Card, and the following precis of our Journey through the 'Twenty-Two Steps of the Process of Self-Creation', <u>via</u> the Sacred Alphabet, Astrology, and Tarot, show the Cards in the original order of the Sacred Letters in the '*Sefer Yetzirah*'. But we must remember that Tarot may be of Egyptian origin, which emulates the Journey of a Pharaoh with the Sun through the Underworld to the Afterlife, and is not based on the

Phoenician Alphabet, even though it reveals the path of our own Inner Journey to our Divine Destination (*destiny*). But if, like a Pharaoh, we believe it is our Divine Birth Right to Rule our own Kingdom in partnership with the Magical Star Seed within our Heart, we will always be preserved and protected until we become the 'Creator' of our own Paradise on Earth through our 'Knowledge of Magic' Inherited by Humanity from our Celestial Ancestors.

Hence, we now realise the physical world is based on the stories we tell, and believe are 'true', and we only experience our own self-image in this world of shadows, which disappears when we no longer react to what appears to be happening around us. And the Tarot Cards can be used to devise new stories, by laying the cards in the order which represent the story that we desire to be 'true', and then living as though this story, or prediction, were already our 'reality', until our 'New Identity' is revealed in our world.

Tarot Cards, like all forms of Prediction, rely on the fact that Humanity is One Whole Being of Pure Light, and we have within us all vibrations that can possibly be experienced by any individual person. And since we have the ability to feel any sensation, we can become impressed by the sensations of another person, or can impress our own vibration on someone else. And when both parties agree to the Prediction, it will come true in the world of Shadows.

The Twenty-Two Steps of the Process of Self-Creation

Our Journey begins with the Mother Letter **AL,** which signifies the Ethereal Element of Air, and the feeling of being 'Nothing' that induces the sensation of Empowerment, and gives birth to our 'Consciousness'. And the first three States of Consciousness, which are **BET** *(Life),* **GAM** *(Heaven),* and **DAL** *(Earth),* are often all that the majority of Humanity are capable of experiencing, until we begin to develop the Virtues of the Zodiac, represented by the Signs: **Aries (HEY)** *Sight;* **Taurus (VAV)** *Hearing;* **Gemini (ZAN)** *Smell;* **Cancer (HHETS)** *Speech;* **Leo (THET)** *Taste;* **Virgo (YAD)** *Action (Touch).* And once these Virtues have been assimilated in our body, our physical senses begin to experience much more than what is seen in the physical world.

For when we attain the Conscious State of **KAPH,** we appreciate the the Vital Energy which is within and all around us, and we become aware of the 'Law of the Universe', and the Virtue of **Libra (LAM)** that is our *Coition or Coalition* with our Inner Spirit. We then understand the function of the Mother Letter **MAH,** which is the Mysterious Ethereal Element of Water, followed by the Virtues of **Scorpio (NUN)** *Regeneration,* **Sagittarius (SIN)** *Modification,* and **Capricorn (AYIN)** *Humour.* Hence, now having attained the Consciousness of Prophecy with the Letter **PEY,** we assimilate the

Virtues of **Aquarius (TSAD)** *Thought,* and **Pisces (QUPH)** *Sleep.*
And nearing the end of our Journey we become Conscious of our
Magical Heritage with the Letter **RESH,** before being Re-formed
and Re-born with the Mother Letter **SHIN,** which represents the
Ethereal Element of Fire. Thus, the 'Process of Self-Creation' is now
Complete as we reach our Divine Destination, having attained the
Enlightened Conscious State of the Letter **TAV.**

The Twenty-Two Letters of the Sacred Phoenician Alphabet are
shown here in sequence from **AL** through to **TAW.** The headings
of the **Three Mother Letters are in bold type**, the *Seven Stages of
Consciousness are in italics,* and the Twelve Virtues of the Zodiac are
in normal print. The Tarot Cards are shown in the same sequence
as the Sacred Phoenician Sacred Letters, and not in the order they
usually appear today. Words which are written in bold capital
letters, are the authors own interpretation, and might be helpful
when considering the original Purpose and Function of each Letter;
since these verbs suggest what action is needed to experience the
vibration of each Sacred Symbol.

Through this 'Process of Self-Creation', while on our Inner Journey
from Embryo to Enlightenment, we will become all that we are
capable of being by devising our own 'Life Story', which is only
limited by our conscious perception of our own Self-Identity.

AL- A, Silent

'ALIGN'

'To Induce the Sensation of 'Empowerment'
OX – Strong Authority –Alignment – Power - Light
1st Mother Letter: Ethereal Element of Air
(the Magical Light in the Air which Empowers our Word)

Before 'Creation' began 'Nothing' existed in the 'Womb of the Mother God-dess', or 'Cosmic Ocean', represented by the first Letter **AL**, and the Ethereal Element of Air. And according to the Phoenicians, **AL** is symbolised by an **Ox** because when two oxen are yoked together the Potential Power and Strength available is much greater than the sum of the parts. The Letter **AL** is also synonymous with the androgynous, Almighty Power/s of *Elohiym*, '*EL*', which is plural in form but with a singular connotation, and is the Ineffable, Magical Light which is evident in the Universe when two, (*Sensation and Knowledge*), are Aligned together in Agreement; thus, the symbol of the Ox 𐤀 was later changed to 𐤗. However, the Universe is in Chaos until the Almighty '*EL*' Declares that 'Pure Magical Light Exists'. And Light is the Pure Consciousness of the Word through which the potential of All Life is Immaculately 'Conceived', but is not yet 'Created'. Thus, when we are centred in the Silence of our Heart we are as 'Nothing', until we are Self-Empowered through the sensation of desire arising within us, and we Speak the Word to Declare that we now 'exist' in the form of our fulfilled desire; for Magical Power is in the Air we breathe, and the Words we Speak. Hence, all Words have Power, but it is our Vision, and Intention when Speaking a Word, which brings forth the appearance of 'Creation' in our world. Nevertheless, only Pure Ethereal Light is Conceived to Exist Within the Beginning, which never changes form. Thus, all physical appearances are the result of the imperfect perception of Humanity, who are as yet unaware that the Whole Magical Universe is essentially Pure White Light.

The Letter **AL** is associated with **Pure White,** which contains all colours, but none are yet manifest. And **AL** is usually placed on the central horizontal branch of the 'Tree of Life'; since this is the Solar Plexus area of our body where all Magical Power is gathered and stored. However, the Letter **AL** was not represented in Astrology until the discovery of the Planet Uranus, which indicates possible sudden changes in life. And Uranus is now often associated with the colour Pale Yellow, as is the **'Fool'** in Tarot, which represents the Beginning of our Journey, Originality, Innovation, Eccentricity, Audacity, and often Folly. And while feeling the sensation of 'Empowerment' at the Silent Centre of our Heart, we set out on our own Inner Journey of Self- Discovery, to our Divine Destination.

BET (Beit) – B

'BECOME'

'To Become Conscious of Being'
Tent Floor Plan – Dwell Within - Spells - Confinement
(1st Stage of Conscious Development: Saturn)
(Consciousness of 'Existing' in a Physical Body)

On the first Day of Creation our 'Consciousness of Being Alive' is formed Within the Beginning with the Letter **BET**, as we Become aware of Being the Vessel in which the Almighty Spirit now Dwells. Thus, with the Letter BET we form the Pattern of the body that we have choosen to inhabit while on our journey through the world of Shadows, which is impressed on our DNA at birth.

And if we consider the Letters, **D N A**, according to the meaning of Sacred Phoenician Alphabet, we find that **DAL**, which is to Determine our Intention; **NUN,** to Narrate our own Story; and **AL**, to Align with the Magical Light Within us, means to impress our self with the story of our Desired Intention, and to Align with the Inner Magical Light to manifest our intention as a Miraculous manifestation in our world; for all that we ever see in our physical world is the reflection of the sensations that we feel are real within our Heart and Body. Hence, once we Become Conscious of living in the physical world, Heaven Above and Earth Below, appear divided, for we are aware of the apparent Dual Nature of 'reality'.

The Symbol of **BET** resembles a Labyrinth in which we feel lost, and are desperately searching for the way out. The Letter **BET** can also signify our own self-devised Pit or Jail where we are incarcerated. Thus **BET** is synonymous with the Planet **Saturn**, Lord of the skeletal system and skin, and represents the limitation and restriction of energy that is associated with the colour **Black,** which is the apparent absence of all Light. But Light is everywhere in our Magical Universe, and the Planet **Saturn** gives us the opportunity to change our Self- Identity, when we alter the Pattern now Impressed on the cells of our body. Hence, **BET** is also associated with the **High Priestess** in Tarot which symbolises Secrets, Hidden Things, Memories which keep us confined, the Casting of Spells (*forming words to bring to fruition a physical manifestation*), and Passing between the Two Pillars of the Ethereal Inner World of Pure Light, and the physical Outer World of Shadows. And the first State of Consciousness we are aware of when we enter the world of our own darkness, and self-delusion, is Ruled by Saturn. However, the High Priestess in Tarot is usually associated with the Moon.

L

GAM - G

'GRATIFY'

'To Be Conscious of Peace and Self-Satisfaction'
Foot - Walk to the Water – Inner Calm – Wholeness
Second Stage of Conscious Development: Jupiter
(Consciousness of Living in our own Heaven)

On the Second Day of Creation, the Consciousness of Being at Peace in Heaven is formed with the Letter **GAM**. Thus, we walk calmly through the 'Circle of Life' with Self-Assurance while feeling the sensation of Gratification and Peace in our Heart as we continue on our Inner Journey to our Divine Destination. **GAM** represents our Garden in Paradise where all of our Treasures are stored, and only await our acceptance. And once we learn to play the 'Game of Life' to perfection, to which there is only one rule, and that it to feel the Satisfied Sensation of Gratification within us. The Letter **GAM** is synonymous with the Planet **Jupiter**, which signifies Expansion, Preservation, Gratification, Serenity, and Spiritual Inspiration. And **GAM** is also associated with the colour **Blue** and the **Wheel of Fortune** in the Tarot, which represents 'Good Fortune', and the Promise that our Prosperous Journey through Life is already assured, when we Walk with Tranquilly in our Heart and Body .

DAL - D

'DETERMINE'

'To Be Conscious of Establishing our Desired Outcome'
Door – Move the Law– Intention – Interaction
Third Stage of Conscious Development: Mars
(Consciousness of our Intention, which Defines our World)

On the Third Day of Creation the Consciousness of our Interaction with the world is formed with the Letter **DAL** and the 'Law of the Universe' comes into action, which is 'As Above So Below'. And this Law Determines that everything we conceive as an ethereal sensation within us will be reflected below in our world of dreams or nightmares as our 'reality'. For the Law of the Universe ensures that 'As we Sow, So Shall we Reap'. Thus, the Letter **DAL** is the **DOOR** which connects Heaven and Earth and is synonymous with the Planet **Mars** that signifies our motivation and the activation of our desires. However, although the Pure Consciousness of **Mars** only bestows upon humans the Spirit of Courage, Daring, Enthusiasm, Passion, and the Potency to put our plans into action, it is now often associated with malefic connotations, which manifest as aggression and self-destructive tendencies. But theses hostile sensations come from within our self, and bear no relation to the Pure Consciousness of Martian Energy. Thus, it is the Intention behind our words which produces the appearance of either benign or malefic appearances in our world; for all words are formed by the Sacred Letters, which are conceived to be Pure and Perfect Within the Beginning, and therefore cannot produce anything other than Perfection, unless it is our Intention to do so.

The Letter **DAL** is associated with the colour **Red** and the **Lightning Struck Tower** of the Tarot, and once again, similar to our understanding of the Planet **Mars**, the original meaning of this Card has been changed and is now more often associated with the possibility of calamity and destruction in our life. But the original **Lightning Struck Tower** was originally regarded as a phallic symbol, known as the 'Fire of Heaven', and the Lightening was seen as a Spiral of Light which represented the 'Fertile Waters of Life', bringing fecundity and nourishment to the land. **The Tower** is also associated with the 'Tower of Babel' when *Yahweh (Jehovah)* supposedly confused the words of the people so they no longer understood what each other was saying. Hence, Humanity has forgotten the meaning of the original Sacred Letters and Words, which only had benign connotations which were intended to Impregnate the Land with the 'Fertile Water of Life', to bring forth only Fruitful Seeds of Fecundity, Abundance, and Prosperity.

HEY- H, E

'ELEVATE'

'To Experience the Sensation of Pure Light Within'

Raised Arms – Behold the Light

1st Virtue: Aries - Sight

(to only See the Vision of that which we Desire to be 'True')

The Virtue of **HEY** is synonymous with the Sign of **Aries** which represents our Self-Identity, and the **Elevation** we experience when we witness the **Vision** of our desire 'Come to Life' through the Magical Power in the Breath of our Spoken Word. For it is with the Inner Vision of **HEY** that we Define our world; for 'Truth', like 'Beauty', is in the Eye of the Beholder. Thus, when we experience taking part in our own Vision, or Story, we witness our Ideal World Come to Life before our eyes. And Raising our Arms in Praise and Delight, we see our Vision become ever more 'Enlivened' with every Breath we take, when we speak the words which declare '*That I Am*'. The Letter **HEY** is also synonymous with the colour **Red** which induces Movement within us, and the Tarot Card the **Emperor,** who is Master of all he surveys, when he Speaks the Words to confirm his Divine Right to Rule over his Kingdom.

Y

VAV (VOW) – F, V, U, W

'UNIFY'

'To Induce the Sensation that our Prayer is now Answered'

Tent Peg – Join Together

(2nd Virtue: Taurus - Hearing

(to Hear Words which confirm the Possession of our Heart's Desire)

The Virtue of **VAV** is synonymous with the Zodiac Sign of **Taurus** which represents our Possession of our Heart's Aspiration. Thus, as we Pray, we Give Thanks that we are now Connected with the Magical Power within us which manifests our Heart's Desire as a 'reality' in our physical world. And to the 'End of our Story' we must stay steadfast to our '**VOW**', while forsaking all other words, which may suggest that our desire is not yet fulfilled. For our Satisfaction is only Guaranteed when we Hear our Inner Word Declare that we are now in Possession of our Heart's Desire, which is then reflected in or world. For all our prayers are answered when we Hear the Voice of our Soul Mate confirm the 'truth' of our Word. And since our Soul Mate is only conscious of 'Purity' and 'Perfection', our prayers are always answered in an affirmative way. Therefore, our mind is impressed with what we are feeling and hearing, when we are One with our Inner Spirit, and we remain 'True to our Word'.

The Letter **VAV** is synonymous with the colour **Red/Orange** and the Tarot Card the **Hierophant**, which represents our Connection to the Pure Inner Light, when we allow our Divine Celestial Spirit to Speak through us.

⌶

ZAN - Z

'ZOOM'

'To Induce the Sensation of Certain Success'
Harvesting Tool – Reap the Seed– Focus
3rd Virtue: Gemini - Smell
(to Focus on the Smell of the Harvest at the End of our Story)

The Virtue of **ZAN** is synonymous with the Zodiac Sign of **Gemini** which represents our ability to Communicate, and **Zoom** in on the **Zone** of the **Smell** of the Fruits of our Labour; which is the Harvest of the Fertile Seeds that we have sown, and are now gathering. But the Zodiac Sign of **Gemini** also indicates that we may be in 'two minds', and therefore there is a choice to be made. And if we choose to Focus our attention on our Treasures in Heaven, then our world will flourish, but if we choose to continue our Journey living in the world of Duality, then the seeds of our Heart's Desire will perish.

Thus, ZAN represents the Celebration which is now taking place in Paradise in honour of the Mystical Union of the sensations we are now feeling in our Body, and the thoughts going on in our Mind. And as we Smell the Sweet Aroma and Consume the Bread of

Heaven, while Drinking the Wine from the Vine of our Celestial Lineage, we confirm that our Certain Success is already assured on Earth. But we must first Harvest the Mature Seeds which have been Sown and Nurtured within us, even though our Seed has only just been planted. For if we do not Focus on 'Reaping the Harvest' of our fully-grown Seed, by experiencing the Joy of Success in our body, then the Magical Consummation cannot take place within us and become manifest in our world. Hence, the belief that there must be a period of 'Time' between the apparent 'Sowing' and 'Reaping' of our Seed is a delusion of the mind, since everything is happening NOW in our Ethereal World Within us. Therefore, we must stay focused on the Successful Ending of our story, and not be tempted to dissipate our energies in other directions.

The Letter **ZAN** is synonymous with the colour **Orange** and the Tarot Card, the **Lovers,** which indicates that we may have an important Decision to make in life. It also signifies Harmony in Relationships, and the Magical Communion of Body and Mind through our Mystical Self-Impregnation, which is confirmed by our Celestial Inner Spirit as we bear witness to the manifestation of our fulfilled Heart's Desire in the world.

HHETS (cH guttural) - H
'HARBOUR'

'To induce the Sensation of Protection and Security'

Wall – Protect the Stronghold

4th Virtue: Cancer - Speech

(to Speak with Charity Toward Self- and all Humanity)

The Virtue of **HHETS** is synonymous with the Sign of **Cancer,** and represents the Protection, Preservation, and Nurturing of **'All Life'** through our **Speech.** For both our Inner and Outer Words affect all Humanity, and defines the people and experiences that we will encounter in our world; since Humanity is One Being existing in the Womb of the God-dess, and connected through the sensations we are feeling. And when we Speak our word with Sensitivity, and Compassion, we Nurture the Sanctity of All Life, and will receive in return the same Charity from others. For **HHETS** signifies our ability to move Walls and Barriers by the Magical Power which is inherent within our Spoken Word. Hence the Letter **HHETS** is synonymous with the colour **Orange/Yellow** and the Tarot Card, the Chariot, which allows us to move safely and securely through life; knowing that we are Triumphant now having gained control of our self and our world, through the benign intent of our Words.

THET – T, Th
'TRANSFORM'

'To induce the Sensation of Alchemical Transmutation'

Clay Pot – Purify the Mud - Taste the Magic

5th Virtue: Leo, Taste

(to Savour the Taste of Magic in the Air that we breathe)

The Virtue of **THET** is synonymous with the Zodiac Sign of **Leo,** and represents our Creativity and ability to produce descendants. Thus, when we **Taste** the Power of the Pure Magical Light in the Air we are breathing, we can produce the appearance of anything in the world through the Practice of Alchemy. For **THET** is the Magical Light within us which 'Transforms' our Perception of 'Reality' by Purifying the Mud of our physical body. And as we Testify that a Miraculous Transformation has now taken place within us, the dormant parts of our DNA will be awakened in our body, and our world will be mysteriously Transformed by the 'Magical Light' which gives us 'Strength' to Convert all vibrations into new manifestations. And the meaning of the word **THET** is to (Transform), (Elevate), and (Testify) to the 'truth' that an Alchemical Conversion has now taken place within us.

The Letter **THET** represents our Ingenuity, Creativity, and our capacity to Transform all outer appearances by the Testimony of our Spoken Word that is synonymous with the colour **Yellow,** which indicates Innovation and Change. And the Tarot Card, **'Strength'** denotes our Inner 'Power' to alter the Direction of the Life Force within us at will. However, the Tarot Card '**Strength**' is often exchanged with **'Justice'** in some Tarot Decks, which may be an attempt to conceal the truth of the Hidden Power of the Forces of Nature, and to confuse the student at this stage on their Inner Journey. But it may also reveal the Hidden Strength of the Alchemical Process that can alter the appearance of any 'reality'. For our Magical Universe, and everything in it, is constantly changing to reflect the 'truth' of our own vibration.

YAD - I, J, Y

'YIELD'

'To induce the Sensation of Holistic Wellbeing'

YAD (I, J, Y) – Closed Hand – Healing Hand

6th Virtue: Virgo, Action - Touch

(to be Grateful for our Continuous Good Health)

The Letter **YAD** is synonymous with the Zodiac Sign of **Virgo,** which teaches us the importance of Self-Evaluation, and represents the **Miraculous Healing** of all conditions when we are **Touched** by the Light of Perfection within us. And **YAD** is the Closed Hand of Restoration, since it Determines our Continuous Good Health when we 'Yield' to the Inner Light, and feel the sensation of now being in Perfect Health. Thus, through Self-Evaluation we can change the sensation of feeling unwell, to vibrant vibrations of wellbeing by asking the question, "How would I feel if I were in Perfect Health"? Until the Miraculous feeling of Perfect Health comes upon us. Hence, when we Give Thanks and Feel Gratitude for our present Wellbeing, we are Holistically Healed from Within. And all apparent maladies are Healed at the moment we are Touched with the Life Restoring Essence of the Miraculous **Hand of YAD;** for all maladies are only habitual sensations which are repeatedly felt in our body, and are accepted as now being 'real' in our mind. But only Purity and Perfection are conceived to exist Within the Beginning, and therefore Humanity must still exist in this 'State of Purity and Perfect Health' right now, which can be induced as a sensation within us at any moment.

And we can heal others too, when we know that all dis-ease is only a reflection of the vibrations that we our self are now feeling within us. For Humanity is One Unified, Whole Being, and everything which appears in our world is according to our own perception. Therefore, it does not matter how we, or other people become Healed, as long as we are impressed with the sensation of 'Good Health' in the cells of our body. And when we cannot induce the sensation of 'Good Health' for our self, then we must find someone who will devise a story which confirms that we are Now Healed of all imperfections. And this person might be a Healer, Shaman, Doctor, a Family Member, Partner, a Friend, or even a stranger who can bring about a change of perception within them self; for the Restorative Hand of **YAD** works in Mysterious Ways. The Letter **YAD** is also synonymous the colour **Yellow/Green** and the Tarot Card the **Hermit**, which urges us to 'Search Within 'for guidance: for through constant inner self-evaluation we can change any apparent physical condition of self, or others, when we **Yield** to the Inner Magical Light of Restoration.

KAPH (Kaf) – K, C

'COMMAND'

'To become Conscious of Vital Energy and Prosperity'
Open Palm – Subdue and Speak–Wealth/Vitality
Fourth stage of conscious development: Sun
(to be Aware of the Abundant Energy that is Within Us)

On the Fourth Day of Creation, the Consciousness of being in Command of the Vital Energy now flowing through our physical body is formed with the Letter **KAPH**, which is synonymous with the **Sun**, and signifies the Pure Magical Light which constantly Shines upon us, and ensures our continued existence on Earth. The Letter **KAPH** is the Open Hand which Gratefully Receive all the Treasures of Heaven when we imbibe the 'Elixir of Life', which is the Light from the Sun which is freely available, and is converted into Dynamic Energy in our blood and the cells of our body. For the Light from the Sun sustains all life in our world, and is indicative of the Star Seed with our Heart of our Celestial Ancestors, which is present when our Heart first starts beating at around eighteen days of gestation, while we are still in the early stages of development in the womb of our mother.

And as we take 'Command' through our Spoken Word, we are Strengthened by knowing that our 'Word is our Prophecy'. Thus, it is in this State of Consciousness that we become aware of the Vital Energy in of our environment, and that of other people in our world who are only reflecting back to us certain aspects of our own vibration. The Letter **KAPH** ⽔ is often placed on the 'Tree of Life' in Kabbalah at the intersection with the Letter **AL** ⽐ as seen in *Figs. 8 & 9*, which shows the importance of the Letter **KAPH** for the development of our consciousness, and spiritual growth. And when we are conscious of this Vibrant Energy constantly flowing through our body we will reflect the vibration of Abundance and Wealth in our world, and will be rewarded accordingly.

The Letter **KAPH** is synonymous with the colour **Yellow,** as is the Letter **THET,** which signifies change, but now we are Conscious that it is the vibration of our own Word which causes the Magical Light in the Air that we breathe to change our perception of the world, through the Magical properties of the Mitochondrial DNA which is inherited through our mother. The Letter **KAPH** also corresponds to the Tarot Card the **Sun,** which is in a different position than is usually seen in the Tarot, but still represents the same connotations of Gain, Riches, Wealth, and Illumination.

J

LAM - L

'LEARN'

'To induce the Sensation of Love and Harmony'

Shepherd's Staff – Ox Goad– Law

7th Virtue: Libra - Coition

(to Be Truly In Love with our Inner Spirit)

The Virtue of **LAM** is synonymous with the Zodiac Sign of **Libra,** which signifies Balance, Harmony, and Partnerships. However, the nature of the partnerships that we will experience in the world depends on our **Coition** or **Coalition** with our Soul Mate which Dwells within us. For without first feeling the amazing sensation of 'True Love' within our self, we can never encounter 'True Love' in our world. But once the Virtue of **LAM** is assimilated within our body, we reach a turning point in our Journey; since from this moment on we remain in a Close, Intimate Partnership with our Beloved Soul Mate within us, while **Learning** of the Impartiality, and 'Justice, of the 'Law of the Universe' through the Guidance of the Inner Voice of Intuition *(Inner Tuition)*. Thus we realise that the physical world is only the reflection of our own self-conceptions, and that our Inner and Outer Worlds are forever joined together as One. And this is the 'Law of the Universe', which ensures that we will always Reap in the world, the same likeness of the Seeds we have Sown. For what we 'Feel is Real' in our Inner world of Sensation, is Mirrored in our outer world of appearances. Thus, as we 'Learn' that the two apparently separate worlds are Yoked Together as One, we know that Pure Light Concealed in our Heart will Reveal the Perfect Image of our own 'True Love' in the world.

The Letter **LAM** is synonymous with the colour **Green,** and the Tarot Card **Justice,** which relates to the outcome of Legal Matters, Lawsuits, and Marital Contracts. And often denotes a deeper understanding of some of the misconceptions and delusions which no longer serve a useful purpose in our life, and now only upset the Balance of our Equilibrium.

MAH(or MEM) - M
'MIRROR'
'To Reveal the Mystery of Life'
Water - Behold the Mystery– Reflection - Manifestation
2nd Mother Letter: Ethereal Element of Water
'to be aware of our own Image that is reflected in our world'

MAH or **MEM** is the Second Mother Letter, and represents the Ethereal Element of Water, which is the **Mirror of Truth** that Reflects the exact image of all who gaze upon it. But when we look closer, we find that 'Humanity is One Whole Being', and is Totally Immersed in the Water of Life in the Womb of the God-dess. And what we see in our world is only a Memory of the collective sensations that we all experience within us. For Water has Mysterious properties which records the Memory of any vibration with which it is Impressed. And since our body is seventy percent water we continue to hold the Memory of the pattern Impressed on our DNA at birth, unless we can change the sensations that we now feel within us.

In Kabbalah the Mother Letter **MAH** is usually placed on the lower horizontal path of the 'Tree of Life', which represents the womb in the human body, and is the organ of reproduction. The Letter **MAH** and the Ethereal Element of Water were not represented in Astrology until the Planet Neptune was discovered, which is often said to signify misunderstandings, confusion, and all things ethereal in nature. But once the true character of Neptune is understood, it will ultimately lead us to our Enlightenment. For Mysterious Neptune, like the Ethereal Element of Water, is constantly changing in accordance with the perception of the person who perceives it. And the 'Law of the Universe' is compelled to reflect in our world the exact Image of what is now held as a Memory in our Water. Thus no materialisation can take place, unless we have first experienced the equivalent sensation within us, regardless of whether we desire that Image to appear in our world, or not; for as with any Mirror it will only reflect the True Image of the one who looks into it. Hence, we cannot alter the Image in our Mirror, until we have changed our self in some way.

But once we realise that 'reality is not formed in the outer world of appearances, but in the Inner Ethereal World, we will no longer attempt to change our world by physical means, but will alter the Sensations that we now Feel within us. Thus, we must remain vigilant that we do not allow ourselves to be Impressed by stories of others that would produce unwanted conditions in our world; for our **'Magical Mirror of Truth'** will always reflect the same likeness of the vibration with which we are now Self-Impregnated, and will reveal this Image in the World of Shadows.

The Letter **MAH** is synonymous with the colour **Pale Blue** and the Tarot Card the **Hanged Man,** which is often associated with Loss in the material world, until we have the Wisdom to know that everything in our world will appear Reversed, when we alter our present perception. And the lesson we learn from the Letter **MAH,** is that the **Ethereal Element of Water,** the **Planet Neptune**, and the **Hanged Man,** are all representations of the Mystery of Life; since no one actually knows what causes material 'things' to appear in our world. However, we do know why they appear. It is because the world we see is the reflection of the Memories now held in the Water of our body. Therefore, our present perception of our self must be Reversed before we can see our word clearly. Then we will learn that everything, and everyone we see in our Magical Mirror is a Shadow of our self, and only 'appear' to have an independent life of their own.

NUN (Noon) - N
'NARRATE'

'To induce the Sensation of Continual Rejuvenation'

Sprouting Seed - Continuous Movement – Regeneration

8th Virtue: Scorpio - Motion

(to tell Miraculous Stories of Everlasting Life and Immortality)

The Virtue of **NUN** is synonymous with the Zodiac Sign of **Scorpio,** which is often associated with Passion, Ardour, and Obsession. However, it is the Inimitable Virtue of **Scorpio** which endows us with the fortitude to carry on with our Mission to make the necessary Transitions from one state of consciousness to another, regardless of what circumstances may appear before us, even to the apparent death of our physical body. And it is by the re-telling of stories that we induce the sensation of Constant Rejuvenation deep within us; for our stories are Seeds which when Planted and Nurtured will Sprout and bring to fruition a whole new generation of stories which tell of the Everlasting Life of our Magical Spirit. And as our present physical body expires and returns to the dust from whence it came, it heralds the end of our present Life Story, which will be replaced with another Story and a new body to continue our Journey to our Divine Destination. Nevertheless, as the Letter of **NUN** suggests, all Life Stories have a habit of repeating themselves; and if we cross over from this world to the next with the same pattern impressed on our DNA as it was at our birth into this life, we will continue to live this story over again, until we change our vibration and become Conscious of a different 'realty'.

Hence, the Letter **NUN** is the Power of Self-Regeneration through the 'Narration' of Stories that tell of Growth and Immortality. And as we induce the sensation of Rejuvenation deep within our Water and Bones, we feel the emergence of New Life in our body. For the original Seed Sown within us at our Immaculate Conception 'Within the Beginning', conceals the Magical 'Essence of the Never-Ending Story of our constant Regeneration and Eternal Life, which is the Innate Power of Nature that continues forever. The Letter **NUN** is synonymous with the colour **Green/Blue** and the Tarot Card, **Death**, which like the Astrological Sign of **Scorpio** is often misunderstood by the majority of Humanity. For Drawing the Death Card does not necessarily denote our own physical demise, or that of another person, but the death of our present story, and subsequent Transition into a new phase of life. And since the word 'death' consists of **DAL (D)** Determine, **HEY (E)** Elevate, **AL (A)** Align, and **THET (TH)** Transform, 'death' means to **Determine** a different 'reality' by **Elevating** our Vision, and **Aligning** with the Pure Light within us, to **Transform** our 'Identity'.

SIN – S, X

'SANCTIFY'

'To Induce the Sensation of Forgiveness of Self and Others'

Support – Shield from Sharp Seed – Rectification

9th Virtue: Sagittarius - Modification of Anger

('to Adjust all Stories that we no longer believe are 'true')

The Virtue of **SIN** is synonymous with the Zodiac Sign of **Sagittarius,** and represents Philosophy, Religious Beliefs, Higher Learning, Freedom to Travel, and the Adjustment of Stories. For the telling and adapting of our stories, which are no longer relevant to our present desires, was very important in the ancient world; since it is the telling of stories that this world is built upon. However, the story of **SIN** is complex, because its meaning has dramatically changed since its original conception by ancient people. For the simple Sacred Symbol of **SIN,** which represented the 'Tree of Life' to the Phoenicians, was once regarded as a means of Support and Protection against the **Sharp Seeds** that grow within us; which may be feelings of Anger, Revenge, Regret, or Shame and Guilt that result in pain in our body. Hence, the word 'Sin' eventually became synonymous with the 'Original Sin' committed by *Adam* in the Ethereal Garden of Eden, and is now interpreted as 'wrongdoing' to those who believe that both 'good' and 'evil' exists in our world. But the Phoenicians were aware that only Pure Light exists in the Magical Universe, and it is our own deluded perception of 'reality' which makes it appear otherwise.

This misconception of the meaning of the Letter **SIN** is now associated with the 'Original Sin' of *Adam*, who after eating the forbidden fruit from the 'Tree of Judgement', experienced the sensations of 'shame' and 'guilt' in his body. Henceforth, these feelings are Impressed as a pattern on the DNA of all humans who have since been born into the world of shadows. And the greater our reaction to the 'shame and guilt' that we now experience, the more we continue to Impress these ideas our own DNA, and that of subsequent generations, which has caused Humanity to forget our Remarkable Magical ability of Self-Reproduction. But once we Adjust our vibration by chaning our stories, the **Sharp Seeds** of 'shame' and 'guilt' will no longer be active in our DNA. Thus, by Ascending the 'Tree of Life' we will see that all sensations of Anger, Revenge and Regret, are not 'Sins', but misconceptions which can be altered at any moment when we Adjust the Stories that we once believed were 'true'. For like *Adam*, we are Conceived as Perfect Beings of Pure Light, and therefore it is we who choose to tell erroneous stories, and to feel delusional sensations in our body, which were not conceived to exist at our Immaculate Conception.

But thankfully, all stories can be 'Adjusted', before, or even after an event appears to have happened; for nothing which we perceive to be 'real' in our world is as solid as it appears to our present limited state of consciousness. And since we are Beings of Pure Light, the incredible Virtue of **SIN** gives us the opportunity to Forgive all 'Transgressions' we believe we have committed, and those which appear to have been committed against us; for we are always Free to change our vibration, by devising new stories that will change the appearance of our world. Hence, as we Sanctify and Forgive all Misconceptions, they Magically dissolve back into Pure Ethereal Light. Thus, now knowing that we are Free to Adjust all stores which we once believed were 'true', we Reveal the Perfect Ending to our Life Story, according to the 'truth' that we desire to be 'real'.

And as we Ascend the 'Tree of Life', and Adjust our Perception, we see that we do not really exist in the form that we believe we do; for our physical body is only a collection of Memories arranged into solidified patterns which are produced by the Intention of the Words we speak. For all Words are formed by the vibration of the Letters of the Sacred Alphabet which were 'created' from Nothing, Within the Beginning, and therefore are ethereal concepts with no physical substance. However, amazingly, our Words are always fulfilled according to the Intention of the one who Speaks, or Hears the Words. But since all Words are 'Spelled' with the Sacred Letters, which were originally devised to tell the Miraculous Story of a Perfect Humanity, any 'sinful' connotation that is assigned to words, must be in the eye of the one who perceives it is so.

Hence if we examine the word, **'Sin'**, which is 'spelled' **SIN (S) Sanctify; YAD (I or Y) Yield;** and **NUN (N) Narrate**, it signifies that we should **Sanctify our self** as we **Yield to the Healing Hand of Restoration,** and **Narrate a New Life Story** to reveal the 'Truth' about our Perfect Self. Also the word **'Anger'**, which is 'Spelled' with the Letters **AL (A) Align; NUN (N) Narrate; GAM (G), Gratify; HEY (E) Elevate;** and **RESH (R) Realise,** indicates that when we feel **'Anger'**, we are choosing to **(A) Align** with the **(N) Sharp Seed of an old story**, instead of feeling the **(G) Gratified Sensation of Peace in our Heaven'**, until this Miraculous Feeling is **(E) Elevated (R) in our Consciousness Awareness.** For every Magical Word gives the opportunity to forgive, therefore we must change the Story of *Adam* and *Eve*, and all other past stories which continue to prohibit us from 'creating' our own Paradise on Earth.

The Letter **SIN** corresponds with the colour **Blue** and the Tarot Card **Temperance**, which signifies Adaptation, Modification, and the Skill to Blend the Ethereal World of Light with the delusional world of Appearances, revealing a Peaceful and Happy ending to all our 'Stories' and 'Spellings'.

AYIN (Oyin) – A, O
'OBSERVE'

'To Develop Insight and Wisdom'

Eye – Continue to Watch – Attention - Humour

10th Virtue: Capricorn - Mirth

(to See 'Reality' Through the Eye of Discernment)

The Virtue of **AYIN** is synonymous with the Zodiac Sign of **Capricorn,** which represents our perception of the world that we believe we are Seeing, which is more an **Attitude** than it is an action. **Capricorn** also signifies our Social Standing, which is Revealed by our habitual **Observations** that we believe are 'real'. However, what we 'see' must be regarded with **Humour** or **Mirth,** since our world is not as solid as it appears, and it is we who are causing what we see through our continued **Attention.** Hence, the Letter **AYIN** is known as the 'Eye', and is often referred to as the 'Evil Eye'. But 'evil' is in the 'Eye' of the Beholder'; for the word **'evil',** which originally meant, **(E) Elevate, (V) Unify, (I or Y) Yield, and (L) Learn,** implies that whatever we **See,** we are Unified with, until we **Yield** and **Learn** from the Inner Spirit that all which exists is Pure Light and Perfection. Hence, **'evil',** which is the reverse of **'live',** is what happens when we fail to see what we desire to see in our world. Therefore, we should look at all appearances with Amusement, since what we see is our own Shadow through the prism of our own deluded perception. And without reacting we must move our Attention to the Silent Centre of our Heart; for we know that to change the appearance of our world, we must first feel the sensation of Wholeness and Perfection within our self. Thus, we cannot blame others for our present circumstance, since everything in our world is only reflecting back to us some aspect of our present Life Story. And as we 'Continue to Watch', we realise that everyone in our world is an actor in the drama that we have devised, which has shaped the characters of the people who are now in our world. And the only way of dealing with any misconception is to regard it with Humour; for what we Observe in the 'world of shadows' is the image of our own self-reflection, seen in our 'Mirror of Truth'.

The Letter **AYIN** is synonymous with the colour **Blue/Violet** and the Tarot Card the **Devil** which represents our bondage in the material world, until we develop the **Discernment** to understand that what we 'Observe' is the result of our own vibration. And if we look closely at the **Devil** Card, we will see that it represents Self-Deception; for the **Devil** has a wry smile on his face, implying that he may not be all that he seems. And the chains around the necks of the children are loose, and therefore, could easily be removed at any moment that we choose to do so.

PEY – P, Ph

'PROPHESY'

'To become Conscious of the Fertility of our own Prophecy'

Mouth – Speak of the Miracles – Fecundity - Providence

Fifth stage of conscious development: Venus

('Consciousness of our Word as the Prophet of our Destiny')

On the Fifth Day of Creation, the Conscious Awareness that our 'Word', which is the Seed of Prophecy, is formed with the Letter **PEY**, that is synonymous with the Planet **Venus** and signifies our appreciation for Art in all forms, and how we **Relate** to our self and other people. The Letter **PEY** was known as the **'Mouth'** to the Phoenicians, because it is through the **Mouth** that all Prophesies and Stories are told. Hence, **PEY** is our 'Word of Truth' which should only Predict that Miracles are now taking place in our world; since when we tell Stories of Miracles, and Yield to the Pure Magical Light' within us, the Fertile Seed of our Stories and Prophecies will always come to fruition in our world. And according to Kabbalists, depending on the area of the Mouth that is touched by the Tongue when a word is Pronounced, will impregnate our words with different Magical properties. Hence, the Mouth was seen as the Productive Womb of the God-dess, and the Tongue as the Phallus which impregnates the Womb with the 'Fertile Waters of Life'. The Letter **PEY**, is formed by bringing the lips together to form the sound of the Letter, which is known as the 'Kiss of the God-dess' that guarantees all our desires will come to fruition, when the Miraculous Ending of our story is impregnated with the Magical Prophecy of our Spoken Word.

The Letter **PEY** embodies the vibration of the colour **Green**, and is synonymous with the Tarot Card the **Empress** which signifies, Fertility, Fruitfulness, Beauty, Pleasure, and Success. And interestingly, the **Empress** and the **Lightning Struck Tower** have now exchanged places in the order in which they usually appear in the Tarot Cards. For the **Lightning Struck Tower** once represented the Phallus which Impregnates the Land with the 'Fertile Waters of Life', but our understanding of 'Words' was said to be confused by *Yahweh* at the 'Tower of Babel'. Therefore, caution is needed when we tell our stories, or make predictions, since the 'Words' which come from our 'Mouth' are fertile, and when our prediction is accepted as being 'true', then it will appear as a manifestation in the world of the one who perceives it to be so.

TSAD - Ts

'TRANSFIX'

'To Induce the Sensation of Conviction and Certainty'

Man on Side – Door to the Stronghold - Stillness

11th Virtue: Aquarius - Thought

('to be Certain of Our Own Self-Identity')

The Virtue of **TSAD** is synonymous with the Zodiac Sign of **Aquarius,** which represents our Aspirations for Humanity, and our Thoughts. And the Virtue of the Letter **TSAD** is our 'Inner Knowing' that the World of our Dreams is already a 'reality', regardless of outer appearances. Hence, by remaining Still and Trusting in the Magical Light within us, we become 'Transfixed' with the Sensation of our fulfilled desire, until we are One with the Pure Consciousness of our Ideal State. For our Thoughts, or Conscious Awareness is always Captivated by the Sensations we 'Feel' in our body, and we 'Know for Certain are True'. And according to the ancient Masters, a person in this state of Utter Conviction is known as a **'Tzaddik'**; for while appearing to remain perfectly still, a **'Tzaddik'** can manifest the appearance of any 'reality' in the world, just by speaking the Word, and 'Knowing' that what they have pronounced to be 'true' is already a 'reality'.

Thus, having Faith that our Inner Magical Light will bring our desire to fruition, the change which has now taken place within us will become apparent in our world. And although it is the sensations that we feel which impregnates the cells in our body with new patterns of vibration, it is our conscious thoughts which form our world in the Image of how we are now feeling. For when we are in control of our thoughts through our feelings, and are Absolutely Convinced of the 'Truth', of our own Word, Magic appears to happen in our world.

For all words have power, according to the vibration of the Letters in that word. But what is most important is the Desired Intention, and Absolute Conviction, of the one who is Pronouncing the Word. Thus, by remaining Transfixed by the feeling that we are now the person we desire to be, our thoughts will be captivated by the sensations in our body, and will appear as a 'reality' in our world.

The Letter **TSAD** is synonymous with the colour **Violet** and the Tarot Card the **Star**, which gives Insight, and Knowledge of our 'Self', and consequently our world. Thus, when we have Faith in our own **Inner Star**, and not allow our self to be influenced by the stories of this world, we are Blessed with the 'Knowledge of Magic' of our Celestial Ancestors, who have Bestowed upon Humanity the Miraculous Ability to 'Create' our own Heaven on Earth'.

QUPH (Kof) – Q, K
'QUANTUM LEAP'

'To induce the Sensation of Timelessness'
Eye of the Needle – Horizon – Shape-Shifting
12th Virtue: Pisces - Sleep
('to Step Through the Portal into another Dimension)

The Virtue of **QUPH** corresponds with the Zodiac Sign of **Pisces,** which is our ability to transform our Karma, or the self-imposed prison formed by our misconceptions and the pattern Impressed on our DNA at birth. And the Sign of **Pisces** is the final Virtue of the Zodiac that must be assimilated within us before we are Released from the Karmic Prison of our own making. Hence, the Letter **QUPH** represents the continual Rising and Setting of the Sun which reveals to us that we too are constantly changing, and that All 'Space and Time' are delusions that only exist within in our mind. For there is no 'past' or 'future', and everything which appears to be happening, is continually taking place 'Here' and 'Now' within us. Thus, by taking a **'Quantum Leap'** into the Unknown, we Cross Over into a different Dimension where all our Dreams and Desires are Fulfilled. And as we 'Let Go' of all delusions we eventually learn that we can move 'in' and 'out' of any Dimension we choose; since our 'reality' is only the reflection of our own self-conceptions. And we are 'Eternal Time Travellers' moving through a Magical Universe which responds to the sensations that we feel are 'real' in our Heart and Body. Hence, we are free to experience any 'reality' we choose. when we are no longer confined in our own prison.

The Letter **QUPH** is synonymous with the colour **Violet/Red** and the Tarot Card, the **Moon,** which represents Hidden Enemies, Delusion, and Self-Deception, but also the evolution of Humanity as we awaken from our dream, or nightmare, and undergo a metamorphosis. Thus, knowing that the hidden enemy is our self, we cannot blame others for our situation, since everything we see lurking in the shadows is only our own self-reflection. And any Image we see in our world can be changed by altering how we are presently feeling. Thus, the Letter **QUPH,** the Astrological Sign of **Pisces**, and the Tarot Card the **Moon**, all represent our own Self-Delusion, until we are Released from this world of shadows by taking a **Quantum Leap** into another Dimension where we 'let go' of our present delusions and Sleep Peacefully, knowing we have never left Paradise, and all 'realities' are already within us NOW.

RESH - R

'REALISE'

'To Become Conscious of the Magical Universe'
Head – Top – Chief - Inherit – Surrender
Sixth stage of conscious development: Mercury
(Consciousness of the Inner Magic which Creates our 'Reality')

On the Sixth Day of Creation, the Conscious Awareness of our Magical Inheritance is formed with the Letter **RESH**, which corresponds with the Planet **Mercury,** and denotes all forms of Communication and Magic. Hence, **Mercury,** that is considered to be androgynous in nature, symbolises the 'oneness' of our body and Inner Spirit, which expresses through us by the Power of our Words. The Letter **RESH** is known as **Head** that also means **Top, First in Command, Chief,** and our **Celestial Birth Right as Ruler of our Kingdom,** which we Inherited on the Sixth Day of Creation when Humanity is instructed to Subdue, Rule, and Fill the Land. However, **Mercury,** is also known as the 'Messenger of the gods' who can play tricks on our gullible mind; thus, causing much confusion in our Head when we are deceived into believing that our Consciousness can be divided. But once we attain the Pure Consciousness of **RESH**, we become aware of the Wisdom of our

Celestial Ancestors, and the Oneness of all 'things'. Hence, when our Feelings and Thoughts are United as one, and the material Elements of *Earth*, *Water*, *Fire* and *Air* are balanced in our body, something Miraculous happens; for we become a Clear Channel for the Pure Magical Star Seed within our Heart to perform Miracles in our world. And as we Surrender to the Will of the Beneficent Power of the Celestial Mother God-dess of Pure Magical Light, we Hear the Inner Voice of our Perfect Soul Mate Speak through us.

The Letter of **RESH** corresponds with the colour **Orange** and the Tarot Card the **Magician,** which is now placed toward the end of our Divine Journey, rather than at the beginning, as it is in a conventional Tarot Deck. For although at the onset of our Inner Journey, it is always our self who is responsible for what we will experience in life, signified by the Magician, if we are not yet fully conscious of our Celestial Magical Inheritance, we only perform Magical Acts by default, and not with Intention. Therefore, the Magician might be more aptly placed toward the end of our Divine Journey, as it is presented here; for we are now fully aware of our Magical Inheritance, and can choose to produce Magical Acts at will. Hence, the presence of the **Magician** in a Tarot spread denotes that Miraculous Powers are at work in our life, when we have the Wisdom to know that we Rule our world in partnership with the Power of the Magical Spirit of Pure Light which dwells within us.

Thus, when we allow the Inner Voice of our Soul Mate to Speak through us, we have Dominion in our world. But when we believe we are alone, and struggling to find some direction in life, we are open to Subjugation by the will of others. However, at this advanced stage of our Inner Journey we have Inherited the Magical Wisdom of our Celestial Ancestors, and know we are destined to 'Create a Paradise on Earth' for all Humanity. Nevertheless, although we are now always United as One with the Pure Magical Light us, we still have no understanding of how 'Magic' works.

SHIN (Sheen) - S, Sh

'SHIFT'

'To Induce the Sensation of Absolute Liberty'

Sharp Teeth – Dissolution – Freedom

3rd Mother Letter: Ethereal Element of Fire

(Power to Dissolve all Delusions and give birth to New Life)

SHIN is synonymous with the Ethereal Element of Fire which eventually brings an end to all delusional experiences, and replaces them with new opportunities for Knowledge and Understanding. The Letter **SHIN** represents the Sharp Teeth that repeatedly Chew Up and Consume all stories, leaving only the Pure Magical Light as it is Within the Beginning, with which we can 'create' a new story. In Kabbalah, the Letter **SHIN** is usually placed on the upper horizontal branch on the 'Tree of Life' and denotes the end of one life and the beginning of another in a different Dimension. The Letter **SHIN** was not shown on an Astrological birth chart until the Planet Pluto was discovered, and Pluto is known as 'Lord of the Underworld' through which we all must pass before we reach the end of our Divine Journey. But the 'Underworld' is not 'Hell', although it might seem so to many, but the place where we meet our own Demons face to face, and the sum total of all our misconceptions which still need to be addressed before we can fully enter into Paradise. But if we have followed the instructions of the Phoenicians, regarding the 'Process of Self-Creation', we will have assimilated the Virtue of each Sign of the Zodiac, and attained the Pure Consciousness of the Planets, and will now have few misconceptions that need to be dissolved at this stage of our Journey. Hence, we will put on the Tyrian Purple Robe of **SHIN** which signifies our Divine Sovereignty, as we walk through the Flames of Expiration with Courage, until we Feel a 'Shift' taking place within us. And Awakening from our Dream, or Nightmare, we know that we are always Absolutely Free to Be who we Desire to be. Thus, Arising into the Pure Magical Light as a Regenerated Phoenix, we now experience the miraculous sensation of being Absolutely Free, and Completely Transformed.

The Letter of **SHIN** is synonymous with the colour **Violet/Red** and the Tarot Card, **Judgement,** which means that we are our own Judge and Jury in our Life Story, and denotes the End of a Matter, Termination, Dissolution, also the Renewal of Energy and our Re-Birth into a New Life. Hence, the **Judgement** Card depicts a man, woman, and child, in the process of **Resurrection** into Paradise. And our old perception of the world has now disappeared forever.

✝

TAW (Tov) - T

'TESTIFY'

'To Become Conscious of Completion and Wholeness'
Mark – Sign - Cross – Target- Signature - Grace
Seventh Stage of Conscious Development: Moon
(Consciousness of the Light we are Reflecting in our World)

On the Seventh Day of Creation, the *'Almighty Elohiym'* had finished 'Conceiving' and it is left to Humanity to form our own perception of 'reality'. Thus, the Pure Consciousness of Completion is formed with the Letter **TAW**, which is synonymous with the Full **Moon,** that signifies our Wholeness and Ability to reflect the appearance of anything in our world when we are conscious of our 'True Identity'. For we are *'Yahweh'*, the Perfect Son (Sun) of the *'Almighty Elohiym'*, **EL** that can only be seen when the Perfect Son (Sun) Shines Light on the Face of the Full Moon, which was traditionally associated with the **'Art of True Magic'**. And while in this State of Pure Consciousness, we know we are 'Everywhere' yet 'Nowhere', 'Everything' but 'Nothing'; for only Pure Light 'exists' in our world. Hence, the Symbol of **TAW** is the 'Sign of the Cross', which 'Testifies' to our 'Whole Truth'; that 'Nothing Exists' until we Speak the Magical Word to Make It Appear So in our world.

214

And now only being Conscious of Pure Light and Completeness we Celebrate our Divine Communion with our 'Soul Mate in Paradise. Thus, consequently, all desire for the 'things' of the material world has vanished, for we are now aware that we can instantly induce the sensation of any 'reality' we choose. Hence, as our connection with our Inner Celestial Spirit grows stronger, together we 'Create' a Paradise on Earth for a Perfect Humanity; made in the Image the Pure Light which is 'Conceived to Exist Within the Beginning'.

The letter **TAV** is synonymous with the colour **Violet**, and the Tarot Card the **World** or **Universe**, which is often associated with the Planet **Saturn** in conventional Tarot. And the **World** Card represents a Change of Direction, of Perception, and Attainment of the Enlightened State of Pure Consciousness. Thus, eventually we realise that our Magical Universe is constantly changing to reflect the Conscious State of Humanity; since Humanity is the Cosmos, and the Entire Cosmos is within Humanity, and we will continue to 'Exist' in our Ever Expanding, Magical Universe forever. For there are many Dimensions and States of Consciousness that are far beyond our present understanding, which will be revealed to us once we have the 'Wisdom to Know the Truth' about our own Miraculous Powers of continuous Self-Reproduction. Hence, when we have Eyes to See clearly a 'New Reality' opening up before us, we will know that we are the Magical Light within our own World.

SIMS

"Arise, Give Life to the Water, and Arise Again"

Morning Star

'SHINE'

Phoenician Legend also tells of the Unspoken Symbol of '**SIMS**' which is 'Indefinable', and is only known as the Pure Light within the Silence of our Heart, which is the Divine Source of *'True Magic'*. For '**SIMS**' is the Magical Power which Gives Life to the Universe. And when we Feel the Pure Sensation of 'True Love' in our Heart and Body, and Hear it Confirmed by the Self-Knowing Word within us, the Magical Universe moves to Reflect the Vision of our Intention. Hence, the name 'Morning Star' is related to **SIMS,** because having attained this Pure State of Consciousness, we will Awaken one morning and the 'reality' of our Magical Universe will have dawned upon us. And we will know that our Divine Journey will never come to an end; for we are the descendants of Self-Reproducing Star People of Pure Magical Light', who came from the Stars to found a civilisation of Enlightened Beings on Earth. Hence, we are free to experience 'self' again and again at any apparent time or place in 'history', in different bodies, on other

216

Planets, in various Universes, and in countless Dimensions; since the constraints of 'Time' and 'Space' are delusions which only exist in our mind. For everything which appears to be happening in the world around us, is happening within us NOW.

To the ancient ancestors of the Phoenicians the Symbol of **'SIMS'** represented the Pure Cosmic Consciousness of the **Star Seed of Pure Magical Light** which is at the Heart of every individual. Therefore '**SIMS'** represents the 'Cosmic Gene' in our DNA which bestows upon Humanity the Miraculous Power to become whoever we desire; and we are the only living creature on Earth that can change our 'Identity' whenever we choose through our own Word. For Humanity has Inherited the Freedom to reproduce our own 'truth', and therefore we cannot help but 'Cast our own Shadow' wherever we are in our Magical Universe. Hence our 'Stories' and 'Dramas' will continue to Appear, and Disappear for Eternity. And after completing the Twenty-Two Steps on our Journey to Enlightenment', we shall finally reveal our own 'True Identity' in our world of Light.

Conclusion

In this Manual we have learned that the Universe is Pure Energy, and that 'Life' is an ongoing process of Self-Revelation, based on our own stories, which are reflected in our world of shadows. And after comparing the stories of the 'Seven Days of Creation', the 'Mystical Kabbalah, the Art of Astrology, and Tarot, we will appreciate that there is a definite connection between them; since all are teaching us that our 'Truth' is already inherent within us, and that we must give birth to our own 'Inner Light' in the world, through our own Spoken Word. Hence when we are experiencing dramas and situations in life that are not to our liking, we must understand that it is we who are 'creating' these stories; for all we are witnessing in our world is our own self-reflection in the 'Magical Mirror of Truth', which is the physical world of shadows.

Thus, the only solution to our present dilemma is to revise the stories and dramas that now appear to be 'true', and replace them with narratives which reflect our chosen 'Identity', by inducing new sensations in our body through 'Speaking our own Truth'. And even if our present story is based on the memory of what appears to have already happened, or might happen, it does not matter, since the only moment that is relevant to our Life Story is 'Now'. And nothing can happen in our world unless it first comes through us. And so, we must always remember that however

218

unbearable or chaotic the circumstances of our life may appear, we are the only person who can change our situation, by altering the vibrations that we now feel are 'real' within us. However, not for just a brief moment, but by continuously feeling that our 'truth' is 'real', until it becomes a habit and awakens parts of our DNA that have lain dormant since birth. For it is the sensations which we feel in our body that influence the thoughts in our mind, and it is not possible to feel one way, and yet think another. Therefore, the feelings which we persist in experiencing will continue to influence our thoughts throughout life, until we develop the Virtues signified by the Signs of the Zodiac that will allow the Pure Consciousness of the Planets to express their Divine Nature through us. Hence, now having descended into the physical world we bring with us the same pattern of energy impressed as a memory upon the DNA in cells of our body at birth, and we will continue to experience this pattern as our story, until our perception of our 'reality' is changed.

The 'Story of Creation' in the Hebrew Bible, which is written from a patriarchal perspective, suggests that Humanity has now become impressed with the pattern of both 'good' and 'evil' vibrations through the 'original sin' of *Adam* (*moving blood*). However, according to the Phoenicians, only Pure Light is Conceived to Exist Within the Beginning by the androgynous Power/s of *Elohiym* (**EL**) on the Sixth Day of Creation. And it is the Hebrews who told the story of the Son of *EL*, *Yahweh*, who is commanded to subdue and fill the land, and to rule over all living creatures. Consequently, so the story goes, *Yahweh*, Son of *EL*, formed *Adam* from the dust of the ground, to tend the Earth and bring forth the possibilities that are 'conceived', but were not yet 'created' Within the Beginning. But *Adam* fell asleep and forgot his Divine Heritage as a Self-Reflecting Being of Pure Light, and now dreams it was *Eve* (*living*) who appears to be separate from himself, that is responsible for the 'shame' and 'guilt' that *Adam* now feels in his body after eating the forbidden fruit. However, *Eve* is not a separate entity from *Adam*, but his own self-reflection in the world. Thus, now believing that something other than the Pure Light Exists, *Adam* and *Eve* are expelled from the Ethereal Garden of Eden, where they will remain exiled in a barren world of shadows until Humanity realises the Perfection of 'All Things' in our 'Paradise on Earth'; for all that was ever conceived to Exist Within the Beginning is Pure Radiant Light, and all else is the reflection of our own deluded perception.

However, as is Prophesised in the 'Story of Creation', Humanity has inherited the Sharp Seeds of 'shame' and 'guilt', first felt by *Adam* in the Ethereal Garden of Eden. And anything which is Prophesied and is Accepted as 'True' by Humanity, is impressed as a memory on our DNA and will be revealed in our world as a manifestation. But *Adam* will eventually wake up and Ascend into

Heaven when once again we will witness to the Glory of Paradise on Earth; as is revealed by the Story of Christianity. For Jesus the Nazarene, having fulfilled the Prophesy of Isaiah, which told of a Son who would be born from a Virgin, and who will choose 'good' before 'evil', is hailed as *Christ the King*. Thus, *Jesus Christ*, who is the Perfect Son of the Almighty *EL*, is restored to His rightful place as 'Ruler of the Kingdom of Heaven and Earth, and is the 'Saviour of His World'. But the majority of Humanity is still asleep, and dreaming of their own 'shame' and 'guilt' in the world of shadows.

Subsequently, the stories of the Mystical Kabbalah, and Astrology, were allegedly devised by Abraham, to instruct Humanity on how we can return to a 'State of Grace' by connecting the Twenty-Two Paths of the 'Tree of Life' to bring down the Lightning Flash from Heaven to Earth, Thus having attained the Pure Consciousness of our Immaculate Conception, we Inherit the Wisdom to Rule our own Kingdom in partnership with the Power of the Sacred Spirit within us. And throughout our Inner Journey to our Divine Destination we become ever more conscious of the 'realities' of this world, as we gain 'Self-Knowledge' and greater 'Understanding' of our Magical Universe, and the Pure Radiant Light which is inherent within 'Everything'. Hence, the Wisdom of Kabbalah reveals that the Symbols and Sounds of the Letters of the Sacred Alphabet will allow us to change our world by first changing our self. For once we induce new sensations in our body, we alter the pattern of our DNA, which transforms our conscious perception of 'reality'.

The story of Astrology also reveals our Divine Right to Rule our World, once we have assimilated the Perfect Virtues represented by the Signs of the Zodiac and attained the Pure Consciousness of the Planets, which are inherited from our Celestial Ancestors at birth. And although Astrology was first devised to re-connect Humanity with our Divine Heritage and show us the way to 'create' Heaven on Earth, it was later associated with the Pure Consciousness and Perfect Virtues of a Leader who is born with the Divine Right to Rule his Kingdom. And the Wisdom of Astrology is now available to anyone who wishes to know their own astrological pattern which is revealed by the position of the Planets in the Signs of the Zodiac at birth. Thus, the Pure Energy of the Planets and Zodiac Signs, which were originally declared to be Functioning Perfectly Within the Beginning, are still functioning perfectly within us now.

However, the Pure Energy of the Planets and Signs of the Zodiac are no longer perceived to be functioning perfectly by some modern Astrologers. For although it is true that we are each living the story that we perceive to be 'true' from the moment we take our first breath in the world, our story should not be one of restriction, but a Celebration of the Pure and Perfect Celestial Light that is inherent within everyone. Nevertheless, while we continue to tell stories of our personal limitation, we cannot hope to experience the Magical Universe in which our Celestial Ancestors live. Hence, we will continue to exist in our present 'reality' until we assimilate the Virtue of the Zodiac and allow the Pure Consciousness of the Planets to express their Divine Magical Nature through us. But having descended into the physical world of shadows at birth, we bring with us the pattern impressed as a memory upon the cells of our body, known as our Karma. Yet, we have the miraculous ability to change our present vibration, since we are born with a 'Magical Gene' which allows us to transform our self through our 'Word'. Therefore, whatever our personal birth chart reveals about our 'Life Story' can be changed when we choose to feel the sensation that our desire is now a 'reality'; which happens at the speed of Lightning.

It is impossible to say where the original version of Tarot originated but may have been devised by the ancient Egyptians to tell the story of a Pharaoh's Journey with the Sun through the Underworld to the Afterlife, where he is granted Immortality. Thus, as a Pharaoh sets off on an Inner Journey to his Divine Destination, he is faced with many ominous reflections of himself, until he is 'Enlightened', and pronounces himself to be Pure of Heart, and now has the Divine Right to Rule over his Kingdom forever. Nevertheless, a Tarot Card spread can reveal our own personal Life Story, while on our Inner

Journey to our Divine Destination (*destiny*). Hence, we start out as the 'Fool', Innocent and Unaware, and are faced with our own demons until we too are 'Enlightened' and Inherit the Divine Right to Rule our 'World', in partnership with our Perfect Inner Spirit; which to the Egyptians is the Star Seed inherited from our Celestial Ancestors, who are alleged to come from the Star System of Sirius.

Nothing in this world is how we once perceived it to be, since the Magical Universe is constantly changing and only appears to be solid to our present state of consciousness, which is based on our own personal assumptions. Therefore, it is not our parents, our partner, our friends, or the society in which we live that is influencing our world, or ruining our chances of success; for our world is only the reflection of our own self-conception. And although we may be impressed by the prophecies and stories of other people, ultimately it is our own choice if we allow this to happen. For in the end it is our own feelings, thoughts, and perceptions which are the only authority in our life, which can be changed at any moment by altering the present vibrations in our physical body, that will in turn control the continual stream of often unwanted thoughts going on in our mind, until a Whole New World is Magically revealed through us. For while we are feeling the satisfied sensation of our fulfilled desire, we cannot possibly have thoughts to the contrary.

That is why Yogis of the East practice mediation, to still the mind, by experiencing the sensation of 'Nirvana' in their body, which moves their thoughts in the direction of 'Peace' and 'Serenity'. However, most people don't feel the urge to look for new ways of experiencing 'reality' until they come to a point in their lives when they are faced with a dilemma that they cannot understand, or resolve by themselves. And so, searching in earnest for an answer to their heartfelt questions, they are often drawn to some religious philosophy, or the Mystical Wisdom of Kabbalah, Astrology or Tarot. And these teachings all give the same answer in one way or another to our present dilemma; which is that we must first change our 'Self' before we can alter the world in which we live.

We can learn new ways of perceiving our world through understanding the stories of the Seven Days of Creation, Kabbalah, Astrology, and Tarot. But we must bear in mind that these stories, which were originally conceived to reveal the 'truth' about the Magical Universe in which we live, have been greatly modified to accommodate the beliefs and philosophies of the one who is telling the story, until they now bear little resemblance to their original conception. Therefore, we must consider the roots of these stories before we decide on their relevance to our own Life Story. But once we know for certain that all we experience in our world is the reflection of our own self-conceptions, we will no longer blindly accept the stories told to us by others, or what is written in books, instead we will rely on our Inner Soul Mate for guidance.

The Sacred Phoenician Alphabet, which is the 'Root of the 'Tree of Life' upon which all stories in the world are suspended, offers us the opportunity to see our world in the Pure and Perfect State in which it has remained since its Immaculate Conception Within the Beginning. And by embodying the Magical Essence of each Symbol and Letter of the Sacred Alphabet from **AL** through to **TAV**, we go through the 'Process of Self-Creation', from 'Embryo to Enlightenment', until we understand that the Perfect Universe is already Within Us. And no longer entangled in the increasingly complex stories and dramas that appear to be 'real' in our world, our Journey to our Divine Destination becomes a simple process, when we are guided by the 'True Love' of our Soul Mate, which forever Dwells within the Silence of our own Heart.

Nevertheless, this Epic Inner Journey of Self-Discovery, regardless of which route we choose to follow, should not be taken lightly, since it requires determination, perseverance, and wholehearted commitment to understand the message of any Ancient Wisdom Teachings. But as we progress on our Inner Journey, we find that the original message of the Sacred Phoenician Alphabet reveals to us that it is only our present perception of 'Reality' which we need to change to manifest our cherished desires in the world. Therefore, we must eat only the Nourishing Fruit from the 'Tree of Life', and continue to repeat our Miraculous Story of Peace, Health, Wealth, and Success over and over again until it is impressed in the blood and bones of our body, and we 'Know' for certain that it is our 'True Identity'. For once we have 'Previous Knowledge' of the sensation which confirms that we are now in possession of our desire, we move from the world of 'wanting', into Paradise, where all our desires are fulfilled through the Self-Reproducing Mitochondria inherited from our Celestial Mother of Pure Magical Light.

Although we may face many personal challenges while on our Inner Journey to our Divine Destination, it depends on how we perceive, and react to that which now appears to be 'real'. For what we experience in our world, and the people we meet, are only reflections of the Life Story that we have devised. Hence, we are the main character in our personal drama, while our family, friends, and partners are our supporting cast who are enacting the script which we have prepared for them. But since our Life is a reflection of our own personal Story, we have the power to change the people who appear in our world, once we learn to change our Self; since it is through our own personal vibration that we perceive others. And once we stop repeating our habitual stories of doom and despair, which keep us in a state of confusion and limitation, our present dysfunctional world will disappear, to be replaced by the reflection of a Miraculous Story. But only 'thinking' about what we desire to happen, will not manifest as an appearance in our world, until we have entered our Secret Sanctuary in the Silence within our Heart, and have 'Cast our Magical Spell' (*Spoken the Word*) to induce new vibrations which we now desire to become manifest in our world. Hence, when we continue to repeat our story, and live as though our desire is already our fulfilled, we will become 'Consciousness' of existing in this desired state on Earth.

Strangely, we always become conscious of being that which we continually practice, even though we may not want to be it, because our quality of life does not depend on what appears to be 'real' in the world, but our 'Actions' 'and 'Reactions' to our own 'Truth'. For when we are absolutely certain beyond any doubt that we are already the person we desire to be, and we remain in the moment when our desire is fulfilled, regardless of appearances in the world, it will become manifest in our life. Thus, whatever we become, it is because we already 'Feel the Sensation', have 'Spoken the Word', and now See the Image of our own reflection in our 'Magic Mirror of Truth'; which is the physical world of shadows that can never appear as anything other than the reflection of our own vibration, as seen through the prism of our own personal perception.

The Creation Stories from around the world, and the teachings of Kabbalah, Astrology and Tarot, are all conceptions of people who seek to keep the 'Old Ways Alive', by revealing that our own 'Truth' is always within our self. And following the Wisdom of *'Tauutos'*, by continuing to repeat our Magical Story until it becomes a habit, we awaken parts of our DNA that lie dormant, and alter the memory in the cells of our body. For this world is Transient in nature, and when we 'Cast a Magic Spell' with benign intention, we induce new sensations within us, and will then 'Cast a different Shadow' in our world. For when we are Truly One with our Soul Mate in Paradise, we are as Pure as our Virginal Mother, and have no need for any outside influence to impregnate us with our Fulfilled Desire. Hence, as it is Within the Beginning, it will be in the end, for we need only to 'Speak the Word' to confirm our desire is now our 'reality', and allow the Magical Star Seed of Pure Light within our own Heart to work Miracles through us.

Hence, when a man is united with the Celestial Spirit of his Inner Female, he is continually Nourished by the Pure Magical Light within him, and he will become the Ruler of his own Kingdom, naming everything which he desires to become manifest. And a female, after going through 'Maidenhood' and 'Motherhood', is transformed into a 'Crone', which is when she is at her most Powerful. For after the menopause a woman is Self-Impregnated with the 'Wisdom of the Word' of her own Divine Spirit, and gives birth to this 'Inner Light' in the world. Thus, we will have no need for any outer mentor; for like the Phoenicians we will know that Miracles are produced through our devoted connection with the Magical Power of our own 'Celestial Inner Light'. But that is not to say that the manifestation of the stories we see in the world are of no benefit to Humanity, since they reveal to us our present vibrations and subsequent state of Consciousness, which when fully understood will help bring us to a 'State of Enlightenment'.

It was the Patriarch Abraham who allegedly devised the Stories of Creation, Kabbalah and Astrology to teach Humanity that the 'Way to our Salvation' is already inherent within us, when we choose 'good' before 'evil'. And while this may be true, these stories are not necessarily in keeping with the Principles of the Ancestors of the ancient Phoenicians, who worshipped the Undivided, Self-Reproducing, Mother God-dess of Pure Light as being the only Power in our Magical Universe. Hence, this Wisdom is now obscured by the many misconceptions that Humanity now accepts as being 'true'. Therefore, we must learn the 'truth' within our own Heart, to re-gain the 'Magical Knowledge' that will change our deluded 'Perception of Reality'. For when the endings of our stories are infused with the 'Pure Magical Light' of the Beneficent God-dess, we will find a 'Pot of Gold' at the end of our Rainbow.

Our Magical Universe is constantly changing to reflect the memory of our self-reproducing vibration, which can only manifest as a different reflection in our world once we have experienced the carnal sensation of this 'reality' in our Heart and Body. And regardless of present appearances, the Universe is bound by 'Law' to only reflect the vibration we are now feeling, but our limited perception cannot yet see our own State of Perfection in our world. Nevertheless, any story can be changed, before and even after an event appears to have happened, for 'Time' and 'Space' as we know it does not exist, and nothing is permanent in our world of shadows. Therefore, we must pay attention to our words, and feel the gratified sensation of our fulfilled desire, as if it were already our 'reality', until the Perfect Image of our Soul Mate which dwells within us, is reflected in the Light of our Paradise on Earth.

Eventually, we learn that our Celestial Inner Spirit is our Loving Soul Mate, and constant companion who will always respond whenever we earnestly ask for assistance. And the inner conversations we have with our Soul Mate are recorded in the cells of our body. However, as with the Ten Sephirot in Kabbalah, we should not name our Soul Mate, since naming anything confirms its identity, and all names are associated with limited physical conditions. Thus, our Soul Mate, who is Pure and Perfect, should not be confined by any pre-conceived label that will only allow us to express the qualities of the Letters in that name. But when we are in Alignment with our nameless Soul Mate, we are free to become whoever we desire; for all possibilities can now be experienced, and freely expressed through us. For it is not only the sensations in our body which produce the Miracles that appear in our world, but our connection with the Almighty Word of our Magical, Un-Named, Spirit of Pure Radiant Light, which resides within our own Heart.

However, the majority of Humanity is still only conscious of a limited state of existence on Earth, since our alleged 'Fall from Grace' in the 'Garden of Eden'. And this story has been kept alive by subsequent generations who have re-told this story, which is still impressed on the DNA in the cells of Humanity. But we have the ability to 'create' a Paradise on Earth by Ascending the 'Tree of Life', and assimilating the Virtues of the Signs of the Zodiac to allow the Pure Consciousness of the Planets to shine through us and produce apparent Miracles in our world. And even though the Phoenicians probably did not practice Kabbalah and Astrology in the same way as the Hebrews, since their basic belief was that the Magical Universe, and everything within it is already 'Perfect', we can learn much from Kabbalah, Astrology and Tarot. For once we 'Know Our Self' we can alter our 'Identity' whenever we choose, by inducing the sensation of any new vibration within us, and seeing everything as already Perfect in our Magical World of Pure Light.

The 'Stories' discussed in this Manual are 'Legends told by ancient people to remind us of our 'Magical Heritage' of Self-Reproduction, Inherited by Humanity through our 'Celestial Mother', which must be accepted as our 'Truth' before we can experience a 'State of Grace' in our Paradise on Earth. But we are not alone on our Inner Journey to our Divine Destination, for if we remain connected with our Loving Soul Mate, our Journey of Self-Discovery will be one of constant Amazing Revelations and Miraculous Experiences.

As we continue to progress from 'Embryo to Enlightenment', we will realise that there is no 'Absolute Truth', for our Magical Universe is constantly changing. Therefore, to live in our Paradise on Earth we must Walk through Life in Peace and Tranquillity, regardless of what our Astrological Birth Chart reveals about our present Life Story, or the Dramas which appear to be happening around us. And if the sensation of discontent comes upon us, like the Phoenicians before us, we must continue to 'Give Thanks' and 'See' our self as already living in the world of our dreams, while repeating the words to induce only benevolent vibrations within us until our chosen 'Identity' is impressed as a pattern on the DNA in the cells of our body; since the key to learning any 'New Identity' is repetition. For 'Life' is a 'Never-Ending, Mysterious, Process of Self-Revelation', perceived through our own unique vision.

"For we don't see things as they are, we see them as we are"

'The Talmud'

Written version of the Jewish Oral Law originating 2nd century CE.

Note from the Author

Our world is founded upon personal stories, and therefore an extensive bibliography only proves that the author can read, and understand on some level the stories that have been written by others. However, whatever is written in books, which is said to be founded on 'factual' empirical investigation, is only the opinion of the one who now perceives it to be 'true'; for according to Quantum Theory, everything in 'existence' is influenced by the perception of the observer. Also, to include a Glossary which gives the meaning of a word that others believe is true, would greatly influence a reader's understanding of that word. And since all western words are founded upon the Letters of the Sacred Alphabet, which were originally devised for 'Casting of Spells' to reveal the Pure Magical Light of Heaven on Earth, any word which does not convey a benign message of 'True Love' and 'Perfection', is according to the limited perception of the person who is interpreting that word.

Therefore, we must form our own understanding of words, and not be influenced by the pre-conceived ideas of others who may have a limited knowledge of the original connotation of a word, or the Magical Power which is inherent within every word that we speak. Thus, it is better to form our own interpretation of words by looking at each Symbol and pronouncing the sound of each Letter with resonance to induce the original benign vibration of a word in our

Heart. Only then will we have knowledge of the true significance of words. Hence, when we devise our own vocabulary, we can change the context and meaning of any word that we hear spoken by others. And through our own understanding we will create for Humanity a 'Whole New World'; for we are each responsible for the words that we Speak and Hear, which form our Identity and confirm our Destiny. Thus, as with all Spiritual Traditions, we must put away our academic books, and rational assessments made with physical scientific instruments, which can never detect the Pure Ethereal Essence in our Magical Universe. And focus instead on feeling the Sensation of the Ineffable Vibration induced within us when the Divine Sacred Letters and Words are Spoken with Resonance; which our Amazing, Illusive World is founded upon.

For the Wisdom concealed in the 'Sacred Phoenician Alphabet', the 'Stories of Creation', 'Kabbalah', 'Astrology', 'Tarot', and the 'Magical Arts', is only revealed by the 'Word of Truth' within our own Heart, which can never be fully appreciated by the words that are spoken, or written by others. However, ironically, although the 'Twenty-Two Steps to Enlightenment' is enhanced through the Power inherent in Words; Words can never define 'Enlightenment'.

Bibliography

Benner: J. (2004) Virtualbookworm.com Publishing Inc., Texas, USA *'The Ancient Hebrew Language and Alphabet'*

Benner: J. (2005) Virtualbookworm.com Publishing Inc., Texas, USA *'Ancient Hebrew Lexicon of the Bible'*

Benner: J. (2007) Virtualbookworm.com Publishing Inc., Texas, USA *'A Mechanical Translation of the Book of Genesis'*

Brydon: C. (2018) Tredition GmbH, Hamburg, Germany *'Alphabet: The Almighty Word Within'*

Kaplan; A. (1997) Red Wheel/Weiser, York Beach, ME, USA *'Sefer Yetzirah: The Book of Creation'* (revised edition)

King James Bible (2002) Bible First Limited, Bath, UK

N.B. *The present interpretations of the Symbols and Letters of the Sacred Phoenician Alphabet are not necessarily those of the above authors, and Visa Versa.*

Cover designed by Christine Brydon and Edward Adamthwaite:

Whatsme: Designs & Collections | Zazzle.co.uk

Author Biography

Christine Brydon has a BSc. Hons. in Health and Human Sciences, and M.A. Degree from the University of Durham, UK, based on the Anthropology of Counselling Practices, and the Performance of Healing Ceremonies around the world.

Christine is a keen student of Holistic Healing Techniques, Religion, Kabbalah, Astrology, and the Mystical Arts; which she has studied and taught for over fifty years, both in the UK and Internationally. Christine was a Tutor at the University of Durham, a Professional Astrological Councillor, and Holistic Therapist until her retirement over ten years ago. And since then she has devoted her time to researching the origins of the Sacred Phoenician Alphabet, and its connection to Healing, the Stories of Creation, Kabbalah, Astrology and Tarot.

In this second Manual, which is based on the Sacred Phoenician Alphabet, Christine brings together all aspects of her lifelong studies and career, so that we might See our own 'Truth' more clearly. And to encourage fellow seekers on the Journey to our Divine Destination to follow the direction which is already inherent within us; for our own 'Truth' can only be found within the Silence of our Heart.

Appendix

If we are not yet able to induce the feeling of satisfaction within our heart and body, we can ask our Inner Spirit the following questions, which will help us to experience the benign sensations which are related to the 'Sacred Phoenician Alphabet'. And without trying to find the answer to these questions with our logical mind, which may not yet know the answer, we must wait in silence until an uplifting sensation arises within us; thus, we can be certain that we are communicating with our Inner Spirit. Hence, by incorporating these new sensations into our own Life Story, we impress this pattern of vibration on the cells of our body, until our mind becomes conscious that this feeling is our new 'Identity', which will be reflected in our world. This list of questions are only suggestions, and with practice we will form our own questions which are more relevant to our particular situation. For we can induce the sensation of any vibration within us, if we ask our Soul Mate how we would feel if we were experiencing the fulfilment of our Heart's Desire.

AL - Uranus – How would I Feel if I were One with Pure Magical Light?

BET- Saturn - How would I Feel if I were now who I Desire to Be?

GAM - Jupiter - How would I Feel if I were at Peace in my Heaven?

DAL – Mars - How would I Feel if I could Live the Dream of my Intention?

HEY – Aries - How would I Feel if my 'Word' Animated my 'Vision'?

WAW – Taurus – How would I Feel if All my Prayers were Answered?

ZAN – Gemini – How would I Feel if I were Already Successful?

HHETS – Cancer – How would I Feel if I were Always Protected?

THET – Leo – How would I Feel if I could Alter my Perception of 'Reality'?

YAD – Virgo – How would I Feel if I were in Perfect Health?

KAPH – Sun – How would I Feel if I were Infinitely Wealthy?

LAM – Libra – How would I Feel if I were In Love?

MAH – Neptune – How would I Feel if I could See my Ideal Image in the Water?

NUN – Scorpio – How would I Feel if I knew the Secret of Eternal Life?

SIN – Sagittarius – How would I Feel if I Forgave Myself and Others?

AYIN – Capricorn – How would I Feel if I could See the 'Reality' of my world?

PEY – Venus – How would I Feel if my 'Words' could Predict Miracles?

TSAD – Aquarius – How would I Feel if I could Control my Thoughts?

QUPH – Pisces – How would I Feel if I could Travel Through Time?

RESH – Mercury – How would I Feel if I Surrender to the Magical Light Within?

SHIN – Pluto – How would I Feel if I were Absolutely Free?

TAW – Moon – How would I Feel if I were Celebrating in Paradise?

Adapted from 'Alphabet': The Almighty Word Within: (*Brydon 2018*)

Lightning Source UK Ltd.
Milton Keynes UK
UKHW010909080223
416610UK00014B/1543